richard Delaney Ph.D.

SMALL FEATS

Unsung Accomplishments & Everyday Heroics of Foster & Adoptive Parents

Published by:

Wood 'N' Barnes Publishing & Distribution
2717 NW 50th
Oklahoma City, OK 73112
(405) 942-6812

When developing family interventions there needs to be protections in
place to guard against misuse of strategies, harm to the child, as well as
insensitivity to the child's history, developmental age, past trauma, etc.
The interventions should always be legal, abide by state regulations, and
be in the child's best interest.

In all cases, interventions should take into account the child's health and
well-being, the need for placement stability, the reduction of stress on the
family, and the healthy empowerment of the foster or adoptive parents.

This publication is sold with the understanding that the publisher is not
engaged in rendering psychological, medical or other professional
services. Any similarity between persons or places presented in this text
and those of any particular reader are purely coincidental.

Cover Design by Blue Designs
Copyediting & Design by Ramona Cunningham
Cover Art and Interior Illustrations by Delores Kroutil, Art House

Printed in the United States of America
Oklahoma City, Oklahoma
ISBN#1-885473-56-7

Publisher's Note

Heroes.

Hmmm.

Fancy suits, cool gadgets, special powers, unbeatable (well almost).

Sounds right to me. But am I writing of Spiderman or your typical foster or adoptive parent. I'm not sure it makes any difference. Maybe the fancy suits and cool gadgets come into question here, but as for all that other stuff it sounds like an adequate description of either.

I know saving the world from sure destruction at the hands of Dr. Meano and his Voltaun Ray sounds pretty different from Bob and Carol teaching little Jimmie about independent living skills. But let's consider the power, commitment, patience, flexibility, and creativity that describe the "superhumaness" needed to save our planet one foster or adoptive child at a time.

What Rick delivers to us in this book is a glimpse at how little difference there is between the small daily feats and unquestioned tasks that come with re-parenting a child in placement or adoption and how they stack up against the feats of Superman. The comparison here isn't to imply that you must be bullet-proof, invincible or perfect to be a foster or adoptive parent, but instead when you add it all up, the difference you make in a child's life is nothing short of its own type of super-humanity.

Small feats, perilous journeys, uncertain terrain and convincing a child you care for them hold hands in the world of foster and adoptive care. As you read the pages of this book, you will see yourself, your actions, and the value, importance and heroics they represent to the rest of the planet.

And while we're speaking of special attributes, we feel it is important to acknowledge the guidance of Rick Delaney. His ability to meet the world of children and their caregivers "where they are" is as enduring as the commitment of the legions of foster and adoptive parents. And for that we'd like to think he's our own kind of hero.

David Wood, Publisher

Preface

This book is about accomplishments, heroics, and foster and adoptive parents. In a nutshell, it's about "everyday heroes." While foster and adoptive parents don't often think of themselves as heroes, they indeed are. Foster and adoptive parents rarely brag on themselves or toot their own horns. Most don't have the time and/or inclination. And, that's where this book comes in. It both brags and toot!

Everybody loves a hero: war heroes, sports heroes, political heroes, heroes in the news. With little thought to danger, a mother rushes into a burning building to save her children. A soldier, dodging bullets, drags a wounded buddy off the battlefield. The pro quarterback scores a winning touchdown as the game clock runs out. All of these heroes perform the nearly impossible, and we award them with headlines, purple hearts, and million dollar signing bonuses.

And then we have the other heroes, the everyday, every-minute-of-everyday, heroes whom I have met over the past twenty years of work with foster and adoptive parents. This book will describe the small feats accomplished by the daily, one-step-at-a-time, cumulative, life-long heroism shown by foster and adoptive parents. I've met these heroes in small towns in the remote West, in the crowded communities of the big city, and—poor me! —even on the emerald islands of Hawaii. Heroism often starts with the placement of the first foster child or with the finalization of an adoption. Once started it may never end. Heroism becomes a lifestyle. One spry veteran foster mother has been caring for other's children for 58 years! With other foster parents it only feels that long!

I have written this book both as a tribute to the foster and adoptive parents I have met and as a testament to what they have accomplished. The tribute and testament are important. But, an equally important purpose is to offer encouragement and hope to those who carry on the day-to-day work in the present. Typically, parents are so close to the daily grind, to the hour-by-hour commitment, that they often cannot see where the path leads and how far they've traveled. And, they question: "Are we getting anywhere with these kids? Is there hope? Will they ever get better?" One foster mom confided, "It's comforting to believe that I am a small player in a divine plan. When it appears that we have not reached a child, we don't know what ultimately will come, what God has in mind. And we worry and wonder." With a smile, she added, "That's why I call my foster children my 'Wonder Kids,' because I **wonder** if I'll ever reach them."

As I began writing this book, I recalled a young couple who came to me, years ago, with their first foster child, another "Wonder Kid" who was a wild-eyed preschooler, hair sticking straight out like straw. The couple said he was "hyper" and attached to no one really and to everyone briefly. This was a **first** sign to me that this boy would demand very close supervision by his foster parents, especially in public. Within minutes of meeting with me alone in my office the boy climbed - uninvited - onto my lap and asked me to adopt him. I was pondering my answer, when he changed the subject abruptly and asked to go to the bathroom. "Alone! I go alone!" he insisted. After several minutes, water seeping under the bathroom door was the **second** sign that this young man would demand very close supervision.

Speaking with the foster parents later, I saw they were overwhelmed. After living a short time with this small child, they doubted themselves and wondered if they could help him. "He's been abused, neglected, and sexually abused. He's got all the symptoms of an attachment disorder. He's angry, defiant, and yet very appealing," they reported. "The Department apologized for placing him with us on such short notice; but they promised he'd live with us for just a few days. It's been two weeks now and the social worker has no other available homes for him."

At the end of our meeting I tried to infuse them with a little encouragement, but I really felt I couldn't drum up much hope. This boy really seemed quite troubled and—I rationalized—would not be living long with these parents anyway. Nonetheless, I couldn't shake the feeling that I could've been more supportive.

Well, with this book I hope I can finally offer more support. The support comes mostly through the vehicle of stories of foster and adoptive parents who have encountered children with large problems, the so-called "Wonder Kids." So, I offer their stories as a long overdue attempt at support to any foster or adoptive parent who is now raising (or ever did raise) a "Wonder Kid."

Overview of the Book

Small Feats has been organized into five chapters.

Chapter One takes the reader into the world of foster and adoptive parents. It gives an overall picture of the range of challenges confronted by caregivers. The foster and adoptive children, for example, whose high-risk behavior jeopardizes their safety and/or that of others. The stories tell of children who demand constant attention, on the one hand; and then children who have no idea about how to ask for what they need or want.

Chapter Two addresses the language of behavior. It focuses on how behavior problems presented by foster and adoptive children communicate much about how they have survived the past and how their world view has been changed by it. This chapter underscores how behavior problems may speak volumes about the child's needs, goals, feelings, and inner struggles.

Chapter Three zeroes in on the child's history and how it shapes his/her development. In this chapter we delve into how prenatal insults, exposure to abuse and neglect, and multiple foster care placements can harm the child. Discussion focuses on the historic roles that foster and adoptive children learn when they come from families of dysfunction.

Chapter Four examines how raising troubled foster or adoptive children results in costs—psychological and emotional—to the family. We hear how taking care of a challenging child can make parents look pretty strange. Important emphasis is placed upon understanding parental echoes, the unresolved issues each of us live with, and how these echoes resonate in our parenting.

Chapter Five recounts the creative, sometimes off-the-wall, parenting approaches foster and adoptive parents have used to reach their troubled youngsters. Among the approaches, we learn how a parent channeled the obsession of a young fire-setter; how another family dealt with the child with blue lips; how one foster family came to grips with the teen-ager who smoked in his room; and how an adoptive couple dealt with a youngster who read hate literature. We end with briefly outlined parenting approaches such as "Parenting By Memo" and use of pre-emptive strikes to help children who won't accept good things in their lives.

(NOTE: In the interests of safeguarding the privacy and confidentiality of children and families, the cases and examples used have been fictionalized and disguised or are psychological composites. Any resemblance to actual, specific individuals or families is due to the fact that trauma and symptoms of foster and adoptive children often form a common, familiar mosaic.)

Richard J. Delaney, Ph.D.
Eagle, Colorado

To foster and adoptive parents
—my teachers—
who opened my eyes to the realities of
foster care and adoption.

Contents

Chapter One

Everyday Heroes in Small Towns and Big Cities

They say that heroes are made, not born. Everyday in small towns and big cities across the country, we see the making of heroes: foster and adoptive parents who meet daily parenting challenges that demand courage. In this chapter we look at the unsung accomplishments and everyday heroism of "parents in the trenches." Picture Sylvester Stallone with a diaper bag. Charlie's Angels with a Medicaid© card.

Foster and adoptive parents grapple with feelings of isolation and aloneness, sometimes living at great distances from support systems. They cope with children who not only drain them emotionally but also endanger the health and safety of their families. They love children who seem bent on making themselves unlovable. Foster and adoptive parents must find ways to protect children who engage in high-risk behaviors and to contend with children who isolate themselves from others. Foster and adoptive parents provide comfort to children who are fearful, emotionally traumatized, physically scarred and for whom learning and functioning are an uphill battle. They help children who do not know how to identify what they need or ask for what they want. Not only do these parents place themselves at risk, but they ask others in the home to live with a certain level of danger. Foster and adoptive parents courageously take on the "throw away" children whom others have given up on, who are deemed un-adoptable, who are described as "institutionalized." They have to endure some professionals and agencies who devalue their input.

"Picture Sylvester Stallone with a diaper bag or Charlie's Angels with a Medicaid© card."

Some of these parents are viewed by their foster and adoptive children as prison wardens, or kidnappers, while abusive past parent figures are idealized. Foster and adoptive parents have the moxie to parent in public under public scrutiny. There is a special courage demonstrated by foster and adoptive mothers who must contend with children who target them with a mixture of love and hate, insatiable neediness and undeserved anger. These everyday heroes are the ones "in the trenches." Let me tell you about them.

Preschool Racing Divers

Traveling in rural Arizona, I met a single adoptive mother who had survived over a year with her young adopted sons, ages three and four. "I had no support after the adoption. I didn't even know that I might eventually need it. And I did need it more than I had imagined."

She explained that when her little boys, two biological brothers, came to live with her, she was a tad puzzled by some of their raucous behavior. She recounted, "At first I thought the boys would be great Olympic swimmers, given their strange physical feats." The woman explained that the boys would spontaneously lurch flat out, face forward and dive on the carpeted floor. They would skid, jump back off the floor and leap flat out again. "They didn't seem to feel pain and didn't mind the rug burns on their tummies." But, the boys took this outlandish behavior dangerously further when they threw themselves down the steps apparently for the fun of it. "It was like living with a young Chevy Chase times two," the adoptive mother joked, though she admitted it wasn't funny at the time it was all happening. And, the self-destructive pratfalls and race diving weren't the end of it. "Then the real scary behavior emerged," added the adoptive mother, "when they started to carve and cut on themselves."

Many foster and adoptive parents feel alone and isolated in their daily, weekly, monthly, yearly struggles with the child. They feel alone after the child has been placed with them. Alone against social services or the court system. Alone with the perplexing, disturbing problems the child comes with. Some would say it takes heroism to live in rural Arizona. However, to live there without access to services for your troubled youngsters, or support from other foster or adoptive parents, or other individuals who truly understand what they are up against... That's true heroism!

Your Hair Thinning?

Many foster and adoptive parents have been assaulted by their children. They have been shoved, kicked, punched, bitten. Objects have been hurled at them, weapons wielded, and threats made and made good. But the next anecdote exemplifies a form of assault that is quite unique and memorable.

A couple in the Southwest shook my hand during a break in the workshop I was giving. They mentioned that their hair had thinned during the early months following the placement of a twelve-year-old foster daughter in their home. "Ain't parenting stressful?" I joked with them, but they weren't laughing. "It wasn't the stress," they clarified. "Joanie (their foster daughter) had been systematically poisoning us." Joanie had laid her hands on a rat poison or some other toxic substance and sprinkled it lightly in the silverware tray. Over time the poison had apparently built up in the parents' systems and resulted in hair loss that looked like mange.

In this case, problem behavior speaks about an underlying homicidal feeling in a child and about her desire to wreck a placement. From time to time all parents think, "This child will be the death of me!" In the above family it almost happened. While most foster and adoptive children are not assassins, their rage at the world lies in wait. Foster and adoptive parents are heroes for permitting an abused child with such anger into their home. While the home they provide for the child is safe, the life that the child offers them may be anything but safe.

> "From time to time all parents think, 'This child will be the death of me!'"

Poop in the Hair

Woody Allen, a comedian and adoptive father, once related his solution to being held up or mugged in New York City's Central Park. "Throw up on your money... Who wants your money now?" Money be-fouled in this way is very unattractive money!

Many disturbed foster and adoptive children find ways of figuratively vomiting on themselves. They foul themselves in ways that make them unattractive to others. Their behavior has a deterrent quality to it. The child who wets his bed, for example, may do so to keep others out of his "stinky" bedroom.

> An adoptive mother complained once to me that her school-aged daughter came to the breakfast table each morning with her hair perfectly coiffed, each hair standing in place. "What are you complaining about?" I asked. She explained that her daughter's hair was styled with fecal matter! What would this tell us about the child's past? What does this communicate?

> The adoptive mother's comment later in the interview spoke volumes about the problem behavior's objective: "You don't want to be downwind from this child!" Her daughter's obnoxious behavior carried a deterrent effect. Who would kiss her on the forehead at the breakfast table? Who would approach her at a time like that?

Dealing with children who make themselves repulsive requires a stubborn courage to hang in there until the repulsiveness goes away. Some children wake up each day with a stiff arm directed straight to the jaw of the foster or adoptive parents. Staying the course with such children, those who make themselves unlovable, takes an act of courage—and faith.

In Search of Mister Good Wrench

Some foster and adoptive children present a supervisory nightmare to their parents. They need constant watching lest they run off alone or with strangers, engage in risky behavior, or get into things they shouldn't. Children get into the medicine cabinet, sniff gasoline, set fires, baptize themselves in the toilet, fall into the neighbors' swimming pool, or, as in the next scenario, dismantle expensive objects:

> *Ronnie, a five-year-old foster boy, could disassemble anything imaginable. Stereo components, computers, printers, expensive toys, and household gadgets—all fell prey to this young kindergartner. And, although Ronnie could take things apart he had not yet developed the capacity to reassemble. "If I've learned one thing about my foster child, it is never to turn my back on him," reported his hyper-vigilant foster mother. "But, others did not take me seriously when I advised them to monitor him extremely closely." As a result of a less watchful approach at school, Ronnie found an*

unsupervised moment during which he scrambled underneath his school bus. He emerged within minutes with a number of nuts and bolts in his greasy hands. After that incident the foster mother referred to him as "Little Mr. Goodwrench."

On duty twenty-four/seven. That's what it's like to be a foster or adoptive parent with children like Mr. Goodwrench. It's never-ending. "Sometimes, you sleep with one eye open," lamented the foster mother. "I hope we can channel his ability to take things apart, so that he can someday put them back together again." It seems that daily heroism is helped by a sense of humor and the ability to appreciate the small steps you are making with a child.

"Sometimes, you sleep with one eye open. Other times you simply don't sleep."

I'm Busy, You're Ugly. Have a Nice Day!

While wandering an outdoor marketplace in Honolulu, I came upon an interesting T-shirt kiosk. There I read a message on one of the T-shirts that read, "I'm busy, you're ugly. Have a nice day!" A cute, if abrasive and hostile, message for anyone with the misfortune to approach the individual wearing this shirt. An interesting comment too on our times. People wearing in-your-face, cloth advertisements. In this case, the message is double: "Leave me alone, but read my sign." Pay attention to me, pay me no mind.

Many disturbed foster children convey a similar mixed message to their foster or adoptive parents. They demand that we leave them alone, yet simultaneously their message attracts us. It's an arm's length relationship.

Heroism in foster and adoptive parents means never giving up on a child, especially the child who needs closeness desperately but routinely fends it off. They fail to communicate, "I need you, Mom. I love you, Dad... I want to live with this family... I know you are on my side." Even so, parents must keep the faith anyway.

When children stiff-arm parents, when they jilt them, rebuff them, and punish those who try to love them, it's hard to "keep on keepin' on." (How old is this author, anyway?) That's when everyday heroism kicks in.

Eyes in the Back of His Head

An abused boy was brought to me by his foster parents for a psychological evaluation. A tall, slender ten-year-old, he had been the victim of horrible physical abuse which resulted in brain damage. When he entered my office he seemed wary and chatted constantly and nervously. He was clearly unsteady on his feet, uncoordinated, and almost tipsy. I wondered if his unsteadiness might be related to the brain damage that he had sustained. He clumsily collided with chairs, a foot stool, my desk, an end table, and overturned a waste basket as he explored my office. With each collision, the boy apologetically remarked, "Sorry chair, sorry table, sorry waste basket." Our young man was not really carrying on a dialogue with these inanimate objects but rather was apologizing to me, the owner of these things he'd crashed into. He also was touching base with me to see if I was angry and would retaliate for his accidents with my things.

Eventually, the young boy sat on the carpet near a window facing away from me and played alone with a board game. I thought that this took a certain amount of trust to turn his back on me—a total stranger and male to boot. (The perpetrator of physical abuse was also male.) Then, I noticed that this child was using the window's reflection to spy on me. In this "rear view mirror" approach, the boy could both keep his eye on me and avoid direct contact. Later, his foster father told me that this boy treated him with fear and wariness too. "He won't let me get near him. Mostly, he won't even look at me. Forget about talking with him, he cowers when I ask him the easiest questions. He's always watchful around adults and seems to have eyes in the back of his head."

Children who have been literally burned, backhanded, beaten, betrayed and broken often treat loving parent figures (that is, the foster or adoptive parents) like they are the original abusers. Foster and adoptive parents have to wonder, "What did I do to this child to deserve this?" After what many youngsters have been through early in their lives, they must have energy, tenacity, even bravery to engage life, conquer fears, and trust others. As traumatized children work this all out, their bravery is often matched by and modeled by the heroic qualities in the foster or adoptive parents. Yes, it requires parental heroism to engage the child with eyes in the back of his head.

"Foster and adoptive parents have to wonder, 'What did I do to this child to deserve this?'"

I Can't Have This, Can I?

Many children cannot or do not ask for what they need. We will talk later about "self parented" children—those who do not believe that needs can be met in the context of a parent-child relationship. In this next story we see that some children give hints but make few demands. Understanding them requires that parents pick up on meager clues. Who knew in advance that as a parent you need to be a part-time "super sleuth"?

> A foster/adoptive mother in a support group remarked that it's not just foster and adoptive children who have problems being direct. She reported, "A little girl in my neighborhood used to show up, unannounced, in our kitchen. She had been taught good manners by her parents. While she wanted to ask directly for something to eat, she wouldn't come out with it."
>
> "We always had a basket on the kitchen table full of snacks, fruit, and sometimes candy. The little girl would sidle up to this basket and mention, almost offhandedly, 'You know sugar isn't really bad for you...' She was not actually asking for what she wanted, but she offered a pretty good hint!"
>
> One adopted boy displayed a similar hinting approach, beating around the bush, never really asking outright for what he

wanted. His approach resulted in a mantra, which he vocalized while touching objects that caught his eye. While touching a small trinket, he would reflexively comment, "I can't have this, can I?" Later, while fondling a new, pocket-sized toy belonging to another child, he remarked again, "I can't have this, can I?" Strolling through my office, he tapped upon, gently lifted and inspected objects all the while uttering the comment/question/ hint, "I can't have this, can I?"

The adopted parents pulled their hair out trying to understand what this anxious, beat-around-the-bush child of theirs was communicating. They speculated:

- He knows his limits and has learned not to take other's things.

- He wants something but does not feel deserving of it.

- He has become used to being denied/deprived by the adults around him; he hints at what he needs but does not just come out and say what he needs.

- He doesn't feel his needs can be met "in relationships" and he expects to be disappointed.

- On the positive side, he hasn't given up completely and holds some small hope that he'll get what he wants eventually.

- He builds in his own cushion for a soft landing, e.g. if he doesn't expect anything he won't be disappointed.

There's something heroic about doing what needs to be done, even though we don't know exactly why we are called upon to do it and how it will turn out. Foster and adoptive parents often wrestle with not knowing. What does this child need? Why does this child do this or that? How long will this struggle go on? Will things turn around for this child? What does the future hold for the child and for us? In the above situation the adoptive parents wracked their brains for answers, not knowing exactly why the child acted this way. But they worked daily to help him learn the biblical message, "Ask and you shall receive." Through the parents' daily courage, the child will eventually become courageous enough to ask.

Needles and Pins

An adoptive family approached me with a terrible and terrify-
ing question. "Will our adopted son, Trent, kill our unborn
baby?" It was one of the most unusual and frightening ques-
tions I'd ever been asked. Why would they ask such an omi-
nous question? What could have raised this question in the
minds of two adoptive parents?

The Smiths had adopted their seven-year-old son from a third-
world orphanage. Prior to placement in that institution, Trent
had lived on the streets for a year—homeless, hungry, victim-
ized. Once in the facility, his physical condition improved, but
he was further sexually exploited by older children. By the time
he was rescued by the Smiths, Trent had suffered chronically
at the hands of an unfeeling world.

The Smiths said that for the most part Trent was fairly easy to
incorporate into the family, in spite of language barriers, cul-
ture shock, etc. But about three months after his arrival, the
family pet, a beautiful, loving dog named Sport, began limp-
ing, snarling and snapping at people. A trip to the veterinar-
ian resulted in a horrific discovery: Sport's paws had been
jabbed with needles and pins. Who would have done such a
cruel, sadistic thing to such a loving creature? And, why?

As you may have guessed, Trent was the perpetrator of this out-
rage against the family pet. Evidently, Trent had grown in-
sanely jealous of Sport and the pet's special place in the family.
While Trent had struggled to exist on the streets and in the or-
phanage, Sport had been undoubtedly enjoying a cushy, loving
existence. Indeed, it was Trent who had experienced a "dog's
life" so to speak. For this boy, the contrast between the pet's
lucky-from-day-one-life and Trent's only-lucky-lately-life was ob-
vious and another source of embitterment.

Also related to the targeting of this dog was Trent's strict ad-
herence to a non-confrontational relationship toward the
adult world. His anger was never manifest to larger individu-
als. He never quarreled with his parents. No word of com-

plaint was ever uttered. Instead anger was apparently stuffed, withheld, and secreted away, only emerging toward safe targets, such as smaller children and, of course, the undeserving, innocent Sport.

Courage, bravery, and heroics are not only the domain of foster and adoptive parents. Other children—and pets—in the home are often called upon to live bravely with a certain degree of fear, threat, and sometimes injury. Foster and adoptive parents are often called upon to elicit secret negative feelings from children who fear them. The hope is that children will discontinue hiding those feelings and realize they can safely vocalize them to their foster and adoptive parents. This demands the courage to permit and invite the vocalization of the previously silent, secret feelings of victimized children.

Loving Children from Psychiatric Facilities

A thirteen-year-old girl in the Southwest had lived for two years in a residential treatment center out of state. This was the longest, uninterrupted "home" in which this girl had lived. Her history read more like a travelog than a childhood. She had moved constantly from place to place, living in twenty foster homes and also in shelter facilities, residential settings, and a half-dozen psychiatric hospital placements. It was no small accomplishment that she had been living for two solid years in the current treatment center.

That stability came to a sudden end, however, when a new state program, entitled "Project Homeward Bound," strove to end all out-of-state placements and bring youngsters "back home." A noble concept but driven at least in part by finances rather than the best interests of children.

Placed then in an instate receiving facility, our young lady was to be prepared to live in a foster or adoptive family. But, she apparently had a different idea! Everyday she went AWOL from the evaluation unit, running off grounds and wandering the neighboring community, breaking into cars and shoplifting

snacks at local convenience stores. She was a loner. She refused to participate in the program, using it more as a flop
house where she slept and ate only two meals: breakfast and
supper. (Lunch usually consisted of packages of cheese and
peanut butter crackers stolen while AWOL.) This youth refused to take her medication and smoked pot occasionally to
help her wile away the daylight hours. Returning to the receiving facility each evening, she demonstrated a wide variety
of behavior problems: verbal aggression and physical out-
bursts, sexually provocative behavior, lying and stealing.

While she missed the staff from the out-of-state treatment
center, she shunned present efforts by the receiving facility
staff to connect with her. In summary, she was an "institutional" kid who had been uprooted from the hard-won stability she had finally enjoyed in the treatment center. Now she
was boycotting any attempts to woo her into the present program and eventually into a foster or adoptive family.

The prospective foster/adoptive mother showed up daily to
meet with her, but was rebuffed by the girl. The foster mother
refused to be denied and began packing a lunch for the youngster, complete with cheese and peanut butter crackers, so the
girl could wander the streets with her belly full. Staff thought
this might amount to rewarding her for running away, but the
foster mother replied, "Work with me on this." After two
weeks of lunches the youngster consented to at least meet
with the foster mother. In the resultant meeting with the foster mother and facility staff, the foster mother suggested that
the girl might need to make contact with the out-of-state
treatment center staff members she had come to care for.
The child cried and seemed relieved that someone had real-
ized the grief that she carried. While the staff of the current
program had its doubts about this approach, the foster
mother continued to voice her opinion that the girl would
need to be in touch with them if placed in her home. In advo-
cating on behalf of this girl, a bond was created, and the child
consented to move into the foster/adoptive home.

It takes courage to take on a child with an institutional background because you never know if s/he will any longer accept a family. There's simply no guarantee that the child can ever embrace family life. Similarly it takes

"There's simply no guarantee that the child can ever embrace family life."

a certain brand of heroism to deal with agencies, treatment facilities, and professionals who don't universally accept or invite input from foster and adoptive parents.

When Children Feel You are Holding Them Hostage

In so-called "legal risk" adoptions, children are placed with good families who are given no promise that an adoption will occur. The birth parents' rights may not be terminated. Lower court decisions might be overturned on appeal. Or, delays in finalizing an adoption may drag on endlessly. As a result, the prospective adoptive parents live in emotional limbo, as does the child. What exacerbates the situation is that some children have an undying homing instinct. Curiously, they often want to return to the very home in which they were maltreated.

> In one such case, a foster/adoptive couple reported that their ten-year-old foster daughter, Bobbi, had tried several times to burn down their home. With extra smoke alarms installed in the ceilings, the foster parents felt more at ease. But, the foster daughter sneaked a stepladder into her bedroom, climbed it to disconnect the wires of the smoke alarm, and then under the cover of darkness set fire to the carpet. Only the presence of a hallway smoke detector alerted the foster family.

> Why would Bobbi go to all this devious and dangerous effort? To speed up the process of being removed from the foster/adoptive home and reunited with her birth family? In essence, Bobbi felt like a hostage in the foster/adoptive home. And, she blamed that family for keeping her from birth relatives.

> In addition to the fire-setting issue, the foster/adoptive parents also commented that Bobbi had destroyed any gifts or "creature comforts" given to her since she was placed. For instance,

she deliberately ruined an expensive Nintendo© Play Station by submerging it in a bathtub full of water; and she defaced new bedroom furniture with a screwdriver. Although these acts all smacked of anger, Bobbi studiously avoided showing anger openly, overtly, and verbally. Instead, she hid behind a constant smile—a grinning hostage.

The caseworker felt that Bobbi would never be returned to the birth family, but that was just an educated guess. And, after court-ordered phone calls from the birth family to Bobbi, the youngster expected to be going back home soon. Bobbi was living with an on-going dream of reunification. Ironically, she was aware that her birth parents had not fulfilled their treatment plan focusing mainly on chronic substance abuse. Yet Bobbi clung to false hope and feeble promises from her birth parents. The court system made no determination about finalization, and the unconscionable uncertainty continued.

> "It takes a great deal of bravery to live with a child that views you as holding her hostage."

It takes a form of courage for foster and adoptive parents to live with the dread that at any moment the child may be taken from them. It also takes a great deal of bravery to live with a child who views you as holding her hostage, and considers herself a prisoner unable to return to her birth family. In the case of Bobbi, there was certain heroism in sleeping with a pyromaniac in the house.

Courage in Public Places

A nine-year-old foster daughter threw an unusual temper tantrum on the Chicago "L" subway. She stripped off all her clothes and pitched a naked conniption fit on the floor of the speeding train, much to the dismay of her foster mother and father and the surprise of fellow commuters. The timing couldn't have been worse; it was rush hour, and the foster parents were quite preoccupied with the care of six additional kids they had in tow. They tried, nonetheless, to reason with the *fallen girl, but with no success. A surprised, somewhat poorly trained subway cop also tried to no avail. (Note: The man is trained to handle terrorism on public transportation, but could not handle "foster terrorism!") The parents then herded the other children away from the commotion and sat in seats at the furthest end of the train away from their demonstrative foster daughter. Luckily, within minutes, the girl came to her senses, dressed herself, and rejoined the family.*

This is a special category of courage: the guts it takes to go out in public with your foster or adoptive children. A crowded train full of edgy and nosy commuters, the strain of parental responsibility for not one but seven children, and an unscheduled tantrum-in-the-buff. Why can't children restrict their problems to the familiar territory of home and yard? The necessities of parenting dictate trips away from the safe confines of your home and you find yourself under the judging glances of unknown spectators. You're not at home, but you are living in a glass house. I believe it takes a certain heroism (or perhaps temporary insanity) to take kids anywhere in public—to a museum, to a grocery store, or (Lord forbid!) on a moving train.

Cinderella Sans Prozac©

A twelve-year-old, Afro-American girl placed with a WASP-ish foster family had been raised to care for her two younger brothers. She was, in fact, the classic "parentified" child. Aside from the obligation of taking care of those siblings, however, she was "detached," an emotional island with a fence around it. The foster mother described this preadolescent as moody, unhappy, living the life of a victim, always feeling put-upon, used, and overworked. The foster father asserted, "Yet, she is the one who assigns the chores to herself. We don't expect it of her. It's like living with Cinderella without her Prozac©." And, what made it worse was the effect on the foster mother, who felt like the "bad guy," blamed by this child for all that she suffered in her earlier years. It didn't help that the child told everyone at school and in the neighborhood, "She treats me like a slave. She thinks she is better than me, because I'm black."

The history of this modern day Cinderella showed that she was foisted with premature responsibilities in her family of origin. For example, not only was she saddled with taking care of younger kids, she was punished when they became too noisy. She also took on the responsibility of all the major household chores, including cooking and laundry, when she was only a kindergartner.

Foster and adoptive mothers are so often targeted by children's anger that they've been called "scape-moms." They have unfortunately inherited negative feelings the child harbors toward past mother figures. In the midst of this, there's a specific courage demanded of foster and adoptive moms who are so unfairly blamed. It takes extraordinary heroism to be misunderstood by the child and others within and outside the family, and to proceed anyway with the task of loving the child.

Summary Remarks:

Foster and adoptive parents and other family members are called upon to be everyday heroes. Much of what is done may be done without fanfare, without notice, without medals and honors. This is the nearly invisible heroism of parenting troubled foster and adoptive children day by day. The everyday heroes, as described in this chapter, contend with:

- Isolation and lack of support.
- The hazards of children who jeopardize family safety.
- Youngsters' distancing maneuvers.
- High-risk behaviors.
- The child's withdrawal, rejection, and fearfulness.
- Unclear communication from the child.
- Fears for other family members in their home.
- Family-phobic, institutionalized children.

- Professionals who devalue parent input.

- The public who has little appreciation (how could they really?) for what foster and adoptive families cope with.

- The child's tendency to idealize the abusers and his/her expectations to reunite with birth families.

Foster and adoptive families juggle many or all these issues and bravely parent day-by-day.

In the next chapter we focus on the language of problem behaviors; that is, on what youngsters' problem behaviors communicate to foster and adoptive parents.

Chapter Two

Problem Behavior is Language, Still It's All Greek to Me

We turn now to the challenges faced by foster and adoptive parents who must deal with their children's problem behaviors. After all, one of the most courageous aspects to foster and adoptive parenting is contending with youngster's emotional and behavioral problems. These problems are often the after-effects of the maltreatment the children have experienced. They've survived, but bring their survival behaviors with them into your home. After the honeymoon period, lasting either an hour or a year, these problem behaviors emerge. That's when heroism is a must. Heroism entails keeping a clear head when all Hades is breaking loose. Heroism means not turning tail but rather facing the problems, looking for answers, and finding solutions.

To get to solutions, parents first must find out what the behavior means. Problem behavior, it is said, is really a form of language, communication about the child's past abuse, present needs, and jaded views of the world. Beaucoup courage is needed to hang in there with the child while you find out what the behavior problems mean. After the meaning is clear, the solutions more easily emerge. Until the meaning emerges, courage must prevail.

"Problem behavior is really a form of language, communication about the child's past abuse, present needs, and jaded views of the world."

Now we turn to situations that typify the problem behaviors. We learn about a child who urinated in bottles rather than in the toilet. Another child who returned from the neighbor's house with blisters covering her lips. A third child who laid under a dog catching its drool in his mouth. And then there is the child who spontaneously pulled out a couple of permanent teeth. Also included are a teenager who carved on her arms and legs, a child who, packing for a short weekend get-away, packed all his worldly goods—every last possession—in garbage bags, a sibling placement where insane jealousy is the dominant emotion, and lastly a child with a terminal sweet tooth. With each discussion we will treat the behavior problem as a form of communication from the child, and ask:

- What does the behavior problem signify?

- What is the child communicating?

- What does this tell us of his/her past?

- What does it reveal about what s/he wants in the future?

The chapter ends with a list of other problem behaviors and possible interpretations of what they might mean.

Urinating In Bottles

Many foster and adoptive parents relate that their children use urine to express feelings that otherwise remain secret. Urine and other bodily wastes often communicate the otherwise inexpressible. Bed-wetting, when not a sign of immaturity or a medical condition, is frequently assumed to be a sign of emotional upset or suppressed anger, defiance, rebellion, control, and/or retaliation. Daytime wetting is often seen that way too, especially if a child deliberately urinates on carpeting, dirty clothes, or clean clothes in a dresser drawer.

> "Urine and other bodily wastes often communicate the otherwise inexpressible."

An eleven-year-old foster son had the unique problem of urinating in bottles. If problem behaviors tell us about the child's past history of abuse, what could this troublesome activity point to? How was his problem behavior a form of language, a communication about his historic troubles?

Possible Meanings:
This child did not have access to a bathroom, so he stored urine in whatever he could find. The child was afraid to come out of his

bedroom at night due to fears of what might happen to him, e.g. he might have hidden in his room from a potential sexual abuse perpetrator. The child stored up anger and expressed this through "pissive aggressive" behavior, "bottling up" anger for latter usage. The child provided a parent or others with urine that would test clean during drug screens or UA's.

Scalding Mouth, Lips, and Gums

A seven-year-old foster daughter, Hermie, came in from out-of-doors with blisters on her mouth, lips, and gums. The foster mother discovered that Hermie had stolen scalding hot food from the neighbor's oven. She wolfed the food down so fast that she burned herself. This was typical of Hermie who has hyperphagia, a condition of eating to the point of becoming sick. Hermie shovels the food in with her hands, mouthful after mouthful, to the point of looking like a chipmunk. She crams her mouth so full that she chokes because she can't chew the food. Hermie has eaten so frantically that she will very frequently bite the insides of her cheeks. Even though she is bleeding and tears are streaming down her face, she continues to eat, shovel, and choke through the meal.

Possible Meanings:
Hermie may have medical/physical problems which could account for her eating problems. Diabetes and depression, for example, can affect appetite. It's possible that Hermie, if on medication, is showing signs of an appetite

change related to that. We also need to consider whether this hyperphagia is related to an early history of neglect, deprivation, and/or malnourishment. Many children with early histories of starvation learn to eat voraciously when food is available. The frantic quality to their eating stems from chronic hunger.

Catching Dog Drool in One's Mouth

A foster mother arrived promptly for Derrick's early morning appointment with me, his psychologist. The mother looked green. "You'd look the same way," she responded when asked if she were ill. She then told a story about the drive over. She assumed that Derrick, her six-year-old foster son was lying down asleep in the back seat of the mini-van. After a few minutes, though, curiosity got the better of the woman, and she adjusted the rear view mirror to check on the little boy. He was lying casually on his back, underneath the massive jowls of the family's Bull Mastiff, catching the dog's saliva in his own mouth.

Possible Meanings:
This child's behavior is so bizarre that one might wonder about thought disorder, early childhood schizophrenia, pervasive developmental disorder, and/or mental retardation. It is also possible, however, that the young boy has been exposed to early maltreatment which might include sexual abuse. In this case you would have to wonder about exposure to the unusual around animals, possible bestiality and/or ritual activities. One other notion to consider is that the child engages in outrageous behavior to provoke a response from others.

Picking On Sores and Other Self-Inflicted Injury

Self-destructive, self-mutilating behavior is not unheard of among troubled foster and adopted youngsters. There are plenty of adolescents who may tattoo, burn, and/or carve on themselves. Younger children will pick at sores, head bang, and bite themselves.

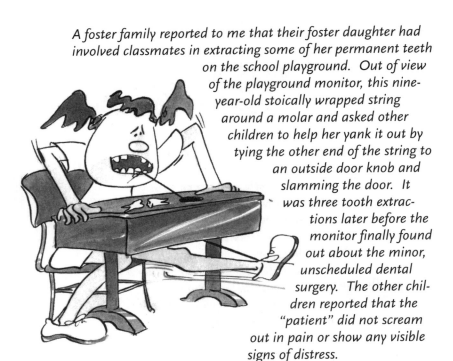

A foster family reported to me that their foster daughter had involved classmates in extracting some of her permanent teeth on the school playground. Out of view of the playground monitor, this nine-year-old stoically wrapped string around a molar and asked other children to help her yank it out by tying the other end of the string to an outside door knob and slamming the door. It was three tooth extractions later before the monitor finally found out about the minor, unscheduled dental surgery. The other children reported that the "patient" did not scream out in pain or show any visible signs of distress.

Possible Meanings:
This child may need to be examined for thought disorder, mental retardation, or pervasive developmental disorder. Oddly, this behavior may be a form of self-stimulation. It may also indicate that the young girl has little awareness of bodily sensations. It could suggest that she is able to dissociate and to therefore be unaware of the pain. Lastly, there is always the possibility that the child has found abnormal ways of seeking attention from those around her.

Pack All Bags

A single, adoptive father was very excited about finally having Timmy placed in his home. To celebrate the occasion he decided to take Timmy camping that upcoming weekend. When Saturday morning arrived, the father asked Timmy to pack because they'd be leaving in an hour on their outing. Timmy disappeared into his room and started packing. After

*an hour the father
wondered why Timmy had not
emerged from his room, and decided to check on him. He discovered that the boy had packed all his worldly goods in two
black trash bags. This was his luggage.*

What does this tell us about the child's expectations? What does
it reveal about his past history with moves? If a child has strange
and idiosyncratic expectations about one area, what can we assume about other areas in his life?

Possible Meanings:
What is likely here is that this child has experienced so much transience, movement, and drift in his life that he expects to ramble
and never come back. When he heard, "Let's go." "We're leaving." "Jump in the car. We're out of here!" he assumed he'd never
be returning. Take whatever you can. Wear as many layers of
clothing as you can. Grab what you want. In general, it may be a
big mistake to assume that foster and
adoptive children view things the same way
you do. What you say, how you say it, who
you are, how you act may all be misinter-
preted by the child. The child's early experiences may powerfully distort how he
perceives events around him.

> "The child's early
> experiences may
> powerfully distort
> how he perceives
> events around him."

Carving Out An Existence

An aging grandmother brought in her thirteen-year-old grand-daughter, Martina, with the complaint, "She's whittling away on herself, on her arms, legs and abdomen." This youngster had begun carving on herself when visits with her birth mother were restarted after a two year hiatus. Grandmother, who had raised this child on-and-off for over half of her life, was again the custodian.

The woman explained, "This child has seen more in her life than many adults!" Domestic violence, sexual perversity, drug parties—this child had seen it all. And, she had been a sexual abuse victim. The grandmother described Martina as a child who rarely showed any negative emotion, and seemed to be totally happy except for the self-mutilating behavior.

"I have to admit that I wish I'd hear some anger from Martina. It just isn't right what she's been through, yet you never hear an angry word from her." Grandmother specu-lated, from random comments, that Martina somehow blamed herself for the sexual abuse and at times regretted having reported it to others.

Possible Meanings:
Given the description of Martina by her grandmother, we have to wonder if she is punishing herself for the sexual abuse she experi-enced. We also have to raise the question: Does Martina feel numb occasionally and need to feel the pain of being alive?

Mom Always Loved You Best

Sibling rivalry can get way out of hand in foster care and adoptive situations as illustrated in the following case:

An eleven-year-old foster son compulsively tried to get the fos-ter parents' teenaged biological daughter in big trouble. First there were the setups: The foster child would steal objects and plant them in the room of the birth child. Then there were the bait-and-switches: He would hit, push, and physically attack the girl, hoping that she would retaliate and accordingly get in trouble with her parents. And finally, there was the sabotage: Cleverly, the foster son unplugged his rival's alarm clock to make her oversleep.

The background, as usual, gives us clues about this compulsive, bitter rivalry. The foster boy was the one child whom his birth family did not keep, though they kept his older siblings. These youngsters had made his life miserable while he was still living at home. In fact, they had tattled on him, set him up to get punished, and otherwise made him look like the "bad child."

Possible Meanings:
The rivalry the foster son has infused into this household grows out of a bitter rivalry that was unchecked in his family of origin. Surely, he learned about insane jealousies and dirty tricks from his older birth siblings. Now, while venting anger in the foster home, he revisits the past on a daily basis. His anger targets an undeserving patsy. In truth, the foster son needs to vocalize anger toward birth relatives who discarded him and kept his siblings. He needs to vocalize anger at past parent figures who failed to rein in his angry, rivalrous older siblings. He carries on a struggle with ghosts, trying to win acceptance at last.

Sweets to the Sweet

A thirteen-year-old boy, Glen, adopted from a Vietnamese orphanage at seven years of age by a childless couple in the Midwest, had a "terminal sweet tooth." A physically malnourished child when he arrived in the U.S., he hoarded, gorged, and fixated on food. In general, over the past six years he had thrived. He mastered the language, excelled academically, and won the hearts of his parents and extended adoptive family. "No doubt about it, he is bonded with us," the adoptive parents asserted. "He is a lovable, sincere, and winning boy. And, he can be so totally focused on other's needs at times." Nonetheless, the food obsession would not relent.

Glen sneaked foods of all sort, but tended to favor sugar—white sugar, powdered sugar, brown sugar. And, he was an "ice cream-a-holic" according to his adopted dad. He ate a gallon tub on the sly one night in his bedroom. He also had wolfed down donuts by the dozen, usually in a favorite hiding spot. When found out, he seemed to feel true remorse, but episodes reoccurred despite the guilt. In addition to problems with sweets, he tended to be hypermanic and mood disordered and had been placed on Lithium. In terms of family life, the adoptive parents reported that the thieving and over-eating of food violated trust and broke their food budget. It also left them without their own favorite foods, and feeling their own brand of deprivation. "It makes me feel like hoarding my own favorite foods," the Dad lamented.

Possible Meanings:
In cases where children are depressed or mood disordered and have food issues, I think it important to have a medical exam to rule out physical causes. Diabetes is one possible culprit. Additionally, certain medications can alter eating habits. Absent physical problems, look at the history of malnourishment as the source of this child's on-going problems with food. While he overcame much of his early upbringing and was a real survivor, the vestiges of early institutional care linger. He was concerned about scarcity of food and access to a commodity—sweets—that could never be taken for granted in his earlier life. Eating in secret points to a continuation of "self-parenting" in a child who historically could not count on the adult world to provide supplies. Lastly, this child struggled to get a balance of altruism and normal narcissism in his life. He often could suspend or disregard his own needs, while tending to the concerns of others.

"Eating in secret points to a continuation of 'self-parenting' in a child who historically could not count on the adult world to provide supplies."

Other Behaviors:

The list of enigmatic behavior problems goes on and on. Foster and adoptive parents witness a myriad of strange actions from their children that often perplexes them. It is beyond the scope of one book to address these behaviors in detail. Briefly, here are some of the most salient behaviors with a speculative comment about the possible meanings of the behavior and why the behavior emerged:

BEHAVIORS	POSSIBLE MEANINGS
Obesity.	Early neglect and starvation.
Blows up a guinea pig.	Victim of child abuse and sadistic torture.
Wets other kid's bed.	History of extreme sibling rivalry.
Burns self on light-bulbs.	Only ministered to when he has hurt himself.
"Bandage child" who looks like wallpaper.	Only ministered to if he has been physically ill.
Makes bomb threats.	History of abuse by and bullying from older children.
Stores things under her mattress until she falls off.	Her life has been chaotic and out of control.
Places noose around baby's neck.	She feels usurped.
Wolfing down food and growling at on-lookers.	Has had to compete fiercely for survival.

continued

Behaviors	Possible Meanings
Urinates in side pocket of back door of car.	Homeless and lived in car.
Hides in caves she builds.	A street urchin who lived by her wits.
Defecates in mother's purse.	Neglected by birth mother.
Refuses to swallow and sometimes smears food all over herself.	History of starvation and failure to thrive.
Refuses to sleep in his bed, instead sleeping in a bag on the floor.	Strong allegiance to birth family and resistance to becoming part of the foster family.
Teenager who gets up in the middle of the night and re-arranges her furniture.	Family history of obsessive compulsive behaviors.
Steals shoes from kids in the neighborhood.	This child doesn't get mad. She gets even, and controls others.
Underwear down the heat ducts or on the roof of the house.	Child has been severely punished around toilet issues.
Always inquires of foster mom, "Have you eaten yet, Momma?"	A history of taking care of his birth mother.
Steals food and gives it to his birth family at visits.	A history of being the bread winner.
Pours flammable fluid on another student at school and lights a match.	Homicidal thoughts toward a sibling who was favored by the birth parents.

continued

BEHAVIORS	POSSIBLE MEANINGS
A foster son who arrives with stolen goods after a visit with parents.	Family shoplifts together.
A preschool-aged foster son can flip eggs in the fying pan and not break the yokes.	Child has been a little parent and homemaker.
Teenaged boy repeatedly makes false claims that he has taken a drug overdose.	Child has learned that only physical problems and injuries get him attention.

Summary Remarks:

Undeterred in the face of risk, confronting dangers known and un-known, and navigating uncharted waters, foster and adoptive parents tackle some very unusual situations. If it is difficult being the average parent, it's truly challenging being a foster or adoptive parent of a troubled child. Foster and adoptive parents often must complete tasks heretofore seen as undo-able or only doable in a hospital setting. They must solve the riddle, crack the code, translate the foreign language of the child's problem behaviors. To do this they must draw upon their special expertise and summon strength and a reserve of courage they didn't know they had.

In the next chapter we focus on how the foster and adoptive family is impacted by the child's history.

Chapter Three

Living with the Child's History—
The Legacy of Pain

Whether they like it or not, parents often live with their foster or adoptive child's history. Though they strive to provide the child with a better life—present and future—they often find themselves mired in the child's past. Coping with the child's history can demand daily heroism.

It's no secret that a child's history from conception forward plays a huge role in later development. Prenatal care (or lack thereof) and exposure to illegal substances or alcohol in utero are the first to impact the child's development. Abuse, neglect, sexual exploitation, and other family dysfunctions significantly impact later development. Once the child has been removed from the abuse and placed in alternative care, any moves from home to home can also damage development. Together or separately these factors can impact how the child develops, what role he takes on within any subsequent family, and what emotional baggage he unpacks in the foster or adoptive home.

In Chapter Three we discuss the damaging impact of prenatal insults, subsequent injury due to exposure to child maltreatment, the negative effects of foster care drift or multiple placements, and the dysfunctional roles that children cling to when coming from skewed families. This chapter explains why troubled children become that way and why living with them is no small feat.

How the Child's History Damages

The history of many foster and adoptive children is tragic. The child may have been unwanted from conception. Once conceived, his mother may have continued to drink and/or abuse drugs. Prenatal care may have been spotty or abysmally absent. After birth, the child may have been given substandard care, e.g. irregular or inadequate feeding not based on his/her needs. Neglect may have been rampant, with the child left to cry unheeded, unwashed, unfed. Or, the child may have been physically abused, bruised, contused, and broken by out-of-control parent figures. Added to that, the child may have been a victim of sexual abuse from one or many, leaving him feeling like a lowly object of gratification for others.

Let's look at prenatal history and histories of maltreatment in more detail. Following that we will discuss the impact of foster care drift on the child. Then we will discuss the development of historic roles, roles that the child has learned based on his/her early relationships.

Prenatal History

Poor prenatal care and alcohol or substance abuse by the mother renders many infants behind from the start. In utero, exposure to illicit substances may result in birth defects, mental retardation, and serious learning problems. The prevalence of methamphetamine abuse is pandemic, seemingly the rage in rural, small-town America. A scourge upon the family, it rivals the crack cocaine epidemic of the last century. Despite the well-deserved concerns about the current drug epidemic, fetal exposure to alcohol abuse actually may produce more serious damage to the fetus. Of course, in many pregnancies there is poly-substance abuse (including undesirable alcohol use) by the mother that may ultimately result in an infant addicted to one or more drugs at birth. One pregnant, teenaged mother in a major metropolitan area was

> "Poor pre-natal care and alcohol or substance abuse by the mother renders many infants behind from the start."

geographically close to services for herself, but did not avail herself of them, mostly because she did not know whether she wanted to go through with the pregnancy. In this situation with conflicting pressures from two family factions, the young woman seemed paralyzed to act. She neglected herself, ran away from home, and abused alcohol and illicit drugs. Ultimately the baby, born premature and possibly with fetal alcohol effects, was taken from the mother. But, by then, we must ask if it is too late for this child to have a fair chance at life.

In another situation, a mother drank a quart of beer every day during her pregnancy, apparently unconcerned about the impact of her alcohol consumption on the child. When confronted about the risks by a caseworker, the woman retorted, "It's my body. It's my right to drink as much as I want. The baby will have to learn I have my rights too." In this instance, the mother's probable alcoholism and personality defects result in an overshadowing and trampling of a child's needs.

This overshadowing of the child's needs may result in Fetal Alcohol Syndrome (FAS) or Effect (FAE), either of which may impact children deeply. In addition to medical problems, children with the less debilitating fetal alcohol effects show behavior problems and thinking difficulties that plague them at home and in school. They can be hyperactive and have poor concentration, lack impulse control, and show central auditory processing difficulties. They may not generalize from one situation to another. Cause-and-effect thinking is compromised and judgment is poor. Thus, they can place themselves in dangerous situations. They have learning disabilities and memory problems. Coordination, balance, and fine and gross motor control may be poor.

In addition, FAE children can be unpredictable, mischievous, manipulative, irritable and emotionally volatile and labile. They seem desperate for stimulation to keep them engaged. They

may engage in risky behavior that compromises their safety and that of others. They can grow to be resentful of the parental structure that they require. They are not in touch with their feelings and may lack empathic skills in interpersonal relationships. As FAE children move into adolescence they may be attracted to conduct problems and delinquent and pre-delinquent behavior. Their parents become increasingly exhausted from having to overregulate, monitor, and discipline these youngsters who find change and transition times extremely difficult and even threatening. These youngsters tend to project blame onto others and are often unable to accept responsibility.

Histories of Maltreatment

Children who have been abused, neglected, and/or sexual exploited are on-going primary victims of their history. Often times, foster and adoptive parents become the secondary victims of that history. The reason for this is that mistreated children view caregivers, themselves, and families in a very distorted, cynical way. The little boy whose nose was partially bitten off by his mother's boyfriend still, many years later, cringed around adult males with beards. The child who had been thrown across the room and against walls, suffered brain damage and chronic anxiety especially around any adult who appeared irritated or angry. One little boy, who as a toddler was heaved through a window pane by his psychotic father, subsequently feared not only father figures but also windows. In each of these instances, the foster or adoptive parents pick up the pieces.

Children who have been physically and emotionally neglected often bear scars that affect them well after they have been removed from the source of injury. For instance, some children have been

fed watered down formula, diluted bean juice, or random table scraps. In subsequent foster or adoptive homes, these children continue to obsess about food, its availability and sufficiency. In such cases the foster or adoptive family deals with the vestiges of childhood starvation.

Children raised in terrifying homes where domestic violence, sexual victimization, and sadistic parenting are common occurrences, cannot feel comfortable in voicing their honest feelings around adults whom they need but fear. One child was tied behind his father on a motorcycle and driven at extreme speeds for punishment. A sibling group was forced to watch as their father kicked the family dog to death. His message was one of terror tactics to teach the children a lesson about compliance and strict obedience to his every command. Children, of course, learn fear by being direct and indirect victims of abuse. When children see their mother abused by men, they learn to fear the men and sometimes to model how the men treat their mother. In the aftermath it is the foster or adoptive family who is left to both calm and re-educate the child raised around fear and violence.

Aside from the scars left by child abuse, neglect, and sexual exploitation, many children have been damaged, traumatized, or confused by poverty, cramped quarters, homelessness, transience, and life on the run. Many know too much about the law, police, jail, and crime. They have lived in homes that have been transformed into drug labs. Exposure to alcohol and illicit drugs, of course, is not restricted to prenatal times. Indeed, many children witness parents in various stages of substance abuse. Drug parties, drug busts, drug sales, and administration of drugs—they've seen it all. One young boy reported that his stepfather coerced him to share injected street drugs with him. Other children have been given drugs to calm them down and tranquilize them into low maintenance behavior around the house. Numerous children report that their first drug experience occurred in the presence and with the consent and encouragement of their parents and other family members.

"Numerous children report that their first drug experience occurred in the presence and with the consent and encouragement of their parents and family members."

Foster Care Drift

Children who have lived in too many homes are often traumatized by the movement and instability to which that subjects them. A child who has lived with birth relatives but has been passed back and forth between grandmother, aunts and uncles, and birth parents has been traumatized often by the transience of belonging. Continuity in care, security in knowing where you live and with whom, and predictability of the attachment figure are absent. In their place is discontinuity, insecurity, and jeopardized attachments.

In addition to the instability within birth families, many "multiply-placed" children have lived in numerous out-of-home placements. The infant who has resided in six different foster homes in the first year of life. The teenager who has been hospitalized frequently and has lived in a number of residential facilities. The sibling group that has blown out of a series of foster and adoptive homes. These youngsters have been subjected to foster care drift.

Much of that drift is accounted for by repeated, unsuccessful attempts to return these children to birth relatives. When that fails, these children are returned to the backstop: traditional foster care. If reunification attempts drag on too long, the likelihood of foster care drift increases dramatically. In one tragic case a sixteen-year-old boy had accumulated 59 placements in his young life. Such a child would be rendered "family phobic" and would be expected to doubt any promise that his present home is "your last home and resting place." Of course, it is the foster or adoptive family that inherits the family phobia, the mistrust of promises, and the permanent sense of impermanence.

The Child's Historic Roles

The child's past is a powerful player in the present. Many foster and adoptive parents assume that if they remove the child from the pain of his past abuse and chaotic world he will behave normally, function happily, and incorporate willingly into their family. At times, nothing could be further from the truth. The past is not swept away so easily. The legacy of pain is not easily dismissed. The child has become the repository of the past. He has learned survival behaviors and, more importantly, historic roles in his family of dysfunction. These historic roles, many of which are exceedingly abnormal, obsolete, and sometimes un-childlike, die hard. In fact, the child's sense of identity is bound up in them.

> "The past is not swept away so easily. The legacy of pain is not easily dismissed. The child becomes the repository of the past."

In my work with foster and adoptive families and their children, I have seen several patterns, common historic roles that have originated in the child's past and stubbornly resist change in the present family. We will discuss these roles next.

1. The In-House Paramedic Role
Some foster or adopted children have learned or earned the role of "in-house paramedic" within past families. In this role the child has become the guardian of health, the watchdog of illness, and the nursemaid to sick, infirmed, psychiatrically disturbed, or substance-addicted parent figures. For

example, one child monitored whether his chronically mentally ill, schizophrenic mother had taken her psychotropic medication, and everyday he counted out her pills for her. Another child hid the liquor bottles from his alcoholic father and checked to see if his comatose, substance-abusing mother was still breathing or whether he should dial "911." A third child brought meals to his bedridden, clinically depressed mother. If he did not play his role correctly, she would refuse to speak to him for days at a time.

The historic role of in-house paramedic often produces a highly anxious, overly responsible youngster who is always ready for emergencies.

2. The Scapegoat Role

In the scapegoat role the youngster has taken the position of the "bad child." He or she becomes the target of family anger, frustration, and conflict. His role is to deflect attention away from other issues or relationships within the home as a way of maintaining a certain balance there. Figuratively, the child takes the blame for others. Biblically, the scapegoat assumed the sins of the community and then was driven out into the desert. In this role the child learns to behave in such a fashion that parental attention focuses on him and his misbehavior. Often the child's temperament, physical or intellectual handicaps or challenges, activity level or physical appearance renders him/her an easy target. Over time, the scapegoated youngster becomes extremely adept at negative-attention-seeking, eventually showing preference for that kind of interaction with others. In neglectful families devoid of parental involvement with the children, the scapegoated child at least obtains negative attention. With parental withdrawal as the norm, this child forces the parents to punish and sometimes abuse him/her. Many children would rather have negative attention than no attention.

3. The Concubine Role

Sexually abused children may assume a role of concubine, that is, a sexual object of gratification. These children often assume an adult-like role, perhaps even a blend of mother and wife. In households where the normal taboos against incest do not apply, older adults may prey on children sexually. The child's value is in being a sexual partner, a sexual object, and/or a surrogate spouse or girlfriend. In many incestuous homes the child may be sexually active with a parent figure, a sibling, or random others in the neighborhood or household. In such instances, modesty may be nonexistent. Sexual activity between parents may be out in the open. Children may be invited into sexual activity with adults or may be encouraged to engage in sexual activity with each other. Eroticism may permeate conversation and interactions, and sex may be an in-your-face behavior with no privacy and no doors. On the other hand, in some incestuous families, sexual behavior is secretive and abuse goes on without the knowledge of the mother or parents. In either case, it is the foster or adoptive family that falls heir to the sexualized child's odd family history.

4. The Companion Role

Some dysfunctional families of origin place children in the role of companion to the parent. In this role the child is expected to save the parent from feelings of loneliness or fears of being alone. Some children are routinely invited to sleep in the parent's bed. Other children are kept home from school when the parent feels depressed or anxious. Still other youngsters become the confidante to a distraught parent who has no social outlets with other adults. In this role the child's own identity is reduced to ministering to the moods of the parent. The parent demands a closeness to the child that reeks of an upside-down dependence. All the while true intimacy between parent and child is absent. The child is symbiotic with the parent, which prevents the child from becoming more independent, confident, and absorbed in his own life, friendships, and activities. Some very young teen mothers see their baby as a plaything there for their convenience and reassurance. When the baby shows more autonomy and independence, during the toddler and preschool stages, this may be a slap in the face to the mother. In some homes the birth of subsequent infants permits the mother to possess the next baby and disregard the toddler, which produces tremendous anxiety in that older child. In some single parent households, the companion child assumes that role when the mother or father has no mate, boyfriend, girlfriend, or lover. When and if the single parent finds another adult companion, the child is relegated to or banished from the parent-child relationship. This child, not surprisingly, becomes hyper-anxious and angered by the rejection.

5. The Parental Role

One of the most common historic roles in children from dysfunctional families is the parental role. The child who dons this role has been described as parental or "parentified." This child, male or female, has learned early-on to take on the parenting of siblings, younger or older. This child, by the age of four or five, may have learned to cook, clean, diaper, baby-sit, discipline and put children to bed. Too good to be true, the child may fold his/her clothes and put them in the dresser. One foster parent reported that the child actually was discovered folding the parent's clothing. In the dysfunctional family of origin the child, often an older child, may become the disciplinarian, expected to keep the other children quiet and behaving while the parent abdicates. If the children do misbehave, run off, or act mischievously, the parental child is held accountable. Thus, many of these parentified children become obsessed with other children's misbehavior and grow increasingly controlling of their behavior at home. This child is attempting to fill a void left by the parent's lack of taking on his/her rightful role, and the child is trying to stay out of trouble by keeping the other children in line. In effect and over time, the parentified child surrenders identity as a child. This child experiences a loss of childhood. While there may be some closeness and sense of satisfaction in raising children, this child has raised them while only a child him/herself. Responsibility replaces spontaneity.

6. The Self-Parenting Child

The self-parenting child has given up any hope that parents will meet his/her physical or emotional needs. Often from neglectful families, these children have learned to take care of their own needs and wants, often secretively. They are invisible, a closed system that does not seem to require anyone outside themselves. Often they are withdrawn, almost a phantom within the household. They eat, but often solitarily. These children may steal and hoard food, addressing needs that parents traditionally take care of. In general these children do not believe their needs can be met in the context of parent-child relationships. They cannot count on adults. Instead they parent themselves. These low profile, low maintenance, self-parenting children make it extremely difficult for subsequent parents, e.g. foster or adoptive parents. They do not vocalize their needs, insist that their needs be addressed, or even accept what the parents offer them. When asked what kind of family they'd like to live with, many of these children reply, "A rich one." To them material goods, toys, possessions, and objects are superior to human relationships.

7. The Victim Role

Some children assume the role of victim, having been historically victimized in the past. (This may overlap with the concubine role, wherein the child assumes the role of sexually victimized child, however, the victim role can also extend into other nonsexual areas.) In such a role, the child feels helpless and hopeless. Commonly the child takes this victim role even further, inviting or eliciting from others the mistreatment s/he expects. There can be a masochistic feel to this role. The child may be doing well at school socially, beginning to fit in, and then it all falls apart because the child cannot handle success. In fact the child torpedoes success and sets things up to be mistreated, often by provoking others to anger.

8. Mixed Role Types

Many children from families of dysfunction and histories of mal-treatment adopt multiple roles or features of several roles. The child, for instance, may take on an in-house paramedic role with her physically disabled father. Additionally, she may be sexually abused by him and thus be forced into the concubine role.

Summary Remarks

Much of the struggle faced by foster and adoptive parents relates to the child's history. The parents cannot escape the child's past but only learn to understand it, face it, and work with it in the present. Pre-natal care or lack thereof, exposure to substances in utero, exposure to mal-treatment, foster care drift, and left-over historic roles often combine to make the child an extreme challenge.

> "Foster and adoptive parents cannot escape the child's past but only learn to understand it, face it, and work with it in the present."

In the next chapter we turn to a discussion of the family life of our everyday heroes.

Chapter Four

The Cost to Parents & Families

Raising a troubled foster or adoptive child brings with it certain costs, some immediately obvious, others hidden. Chapter Four addresses how parents' rosy expectations may collide with the harsh realities of taking on a special needs child. It describes how taking care of a troubled child and adapting to the oddities of the child's behavior shape the parent's own actions. This chapter also discusses how even technically perfect parenting can result in the child's acting out. Our discussion then underscores how some children act out angry feelings by getting even with—not mad at— the foster or adoptive parents. Lastly, major emphasis is placed on echoes from the parent's past that intersect with the child's own ghosts. Needless to say, most children have a way of reacquainting us with our past, our issues, or unfinished business. Troubled children often excel at this reacquaintance process.

"Most children have a way of reacquainting us with our past, our issues, and our unfinished business."

The Empire State Building

A man was standing on the observation deck atop the Empire State Building. Leaning over a bit too far, he slipped and fell. Plummeting past the 100th floor, 90th floor, 75th floor, the man began picking up speed. As he passed the 50th floor, a window washer saw the human streak by and he yelled out to the man falling, "Hey! How's it goin'?" The guy falling yelled back, "So far, so good!"

The old expression is, "It's not the fall, it's that sudden stop that gets you," may apply here. Indeed, many placements are in a free fall from the moment the child enters the home, but the family doesn't exactly realize it yet. Initially, things appear to be going well. Certain things slide by. Other things go unnoticed. Problems are dismissed as temporary. In these families, the adoptive parents might say that things are going passably well. "So far, so good!" they might add, unaware that the free fall may end in disaster, if there is no safety net under them.

One adoptive father, two years after the placement, remarked, "At first things went so well with Sammy that we thought others who had fostered him had exaggerated about his problems—that they had made mountains out of mole hills. Only a year later, we changed our minds! By then, we were convinced that the previous foster parents had mislead us and had underestimated the extent of Sammy's problems. Yes, we were flying high until we crashed almost without a warning."

A Chance Encounter in a Restaurant

I had just sat down at a breakfast table in a Holiday Inn. Before the waiter came by with coffee, a man and woman approached my table smiling broadly and asked, "Aren't you Rick Delaney?" I thought, "These bill collectors are everywhere!" But, they weren't bill collectors. They informed me they were in town from their home state seven hundred miles away, to visit their future adopted son for the very first time. "Where is he now living?" I asked. It turned out that the twelve-year-old boy was living in an intensive residential treatment facility for treatment of youngsters who have begun perpetrating sexually. The boy, a sexual abuse victim, had started to sexually act out coercively on others.

I observed, "That seems like a pretty big problem." The wife responded immediately that the youth was approved by managed care for a five-month stay in the RTC to "fix" his problem. She went on to tell me that they had never had children, let

*alone troubled foster or adopted children. But, they were both
so very excited to adopt this child. I didn't quite know what to
say and sat speechless for a few seconds. I didn't want to rain
on their parade. But the naive couple had me concerned for
their future.*

*After I pulled myself together, I told the prospective adoptive
couple that they should join an adoptive parent support group
post-haste. I strongly urged them to contact a therapist who
specialized in working with special needs adoptions. The
couple walked away not smiling quite as broadly and probably
wondering why I had been so negative. I prided myself on being honest.*

After this chance encounter, I spoke to a group of experienced special needs adoptive parents about it. They did not congratulate
me but confronted me, "Why didn't you tell them the truth? Why
didn't you tell them what it would really be like? Why didn't you
inform them what this could do to their lives?" "Why didn't you
warn them about false allegations?"

> **"It may be a bad
> omen when we need
> to search several
> states away to find
> a home for a child."**

It may be a bad omen when we need
to search several states away to find a
home for a child. Did this couple
have any sense of how troubled this
prospective son was? Had anyone
truly disclosed what they as a couple
might be in for? And, a more general question: when is the proper
time to be candid with foster and adoptive parents? Some say we
shouldn't "scare them away" too soon. Most parents I speak with
say that honesty should begin immediately.

Light Bulbs in Their Pockets

*A very normal looking couple came to my office for their first
visit. The wife sat down on the couch, and her husband began to take a seat next to her, when he exclaimed, "Oops! I
better take these out of my pockets first."*

He then pulled a light bulb out of each of his front pockets, set them on the end table and proceeded to sit. I've seen a few strange entrances, but this really took the cake. At first I hesitated to ask about the light bulbs, but, being a psychologist, I had to inquire.

Then came the unusual explanation. "Our foster daughter, Tilly, has big behavioral problems related to early abuse. She is obsessed with breaking glass, plastic, well, anything breakable. Our house looks like an institution, with screening over the inside of each window. We have child-proofed everything around us to keep Tilly from breaking things that could shatter and hurt her or us. We like to read, though, and so have kept lamps around the house. But, we must take light bulbs with us and screw them in and out before and after reading.

"Once a new bus driver left Tilly at a street corner without us there to pick her up. Wandering down the street, she was approached by a little old lady who saw that she was lost. Tilly did not speak to her and was led to her apartment where the little old lady phoned authorities. While still on the phone she heard a loud crash from the other room. Tilly had butted her head through her picture window."

Foster and adoptive parents, adjusting to life with a troubled child, can sometimes appear abnormal to the untrained eye. Their adaptation to the child's abnormal behavior can be time-consuming, exhausting, and even odd looking. Outsiders may mistakenly assume the family is strange or dysfunctional. To those who never knew the parents prior to placement, these folks may not only be viewed as weird, but as accountable for any weirdness in the child. Foster and adoptive parents are heroes for taking the stares and public glances and going about doing their job.

He Ate All the Worms

One motivated adoptive mom wanted to do some "bonding" with her new son. Fishing, she thought. What could be better? They dug worms from the backyard and carefully planted them in soft loam in a coffee can. They drove to a wilderness area, parked the car, picked up their gear and trekked through the woods to a secluded lake. The mom carried the rods, reels and tackle box, while her son bore the can of worms. After a fifteen minute stroll with Mom in the lead, they arrived at their destination. Setting the rods and reels and tackle on the sandy beach, the mom turned to her son for the bait for the fishhooks. Searching through the coffee can, she found nothing. No worms. And, then she looked at her son's face with dirt traces around the corners of his mouth.

Event the best laid plans run aground or amuck with some kids. Even when parents hike that extra mile, give that extra effort, offer that extra attention, kids may continue to misbehave or even get worse.

Sometimes the behavior even worsens in response to extra efforts at good parenting. Nonetheless, courageous parents doggedly persist in the face of worsening behavior.

Fish Hooks in the Carpet

A foster mother well-known to me for several years, hobbled into the reception area for an appointment with me.

"Where's Bobbi?" I inquired, since there was no sign of her foster daughter.

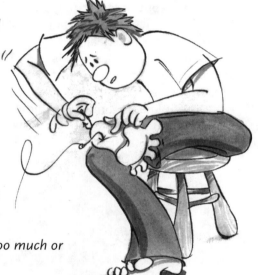

"I'll explain all that in a minute," she replied. So, I asked her to join me in my office, and she gingerly tiptoed back to my office with me. Once seated on the couch, she slowly removed her shoes and followed that with carefully peeling off her socks. The bottoms of her feet were covered with gauze bandages and tape.

"Have you been jogging too much or something?" I queried.

"No," she retorted, "It's from fishhooks!"

As the story unfolded I learned that Bobbi had planted fishhooks in the carpet outside the kitchen. This was during the middle of the night, after all were asleep. She was retaliating for being grounded by the foster mother the previous day. When her foster mom in her usual barefooted way, walked into the kitchen for her early morning coffee, she walked right through a minefield of fishhooks.

"Many foster and adoptive parents feel the child's pain-literally."

Many foster and adoptive parents feel the child's pain—literally. The pain and anguish the child has been subjected to prior to living with a new family come with her. The foster and adoptive parents become "stand-ins." The child can safely vent anger from the past and rage at past caregivers who gave little careto them. (In addition to small feats, some parents have sore feet.) In some instances the children vent the anger behaviorally rather than in words.

Echoes From the Past

A common, but heroic struggle that parents face is contending with children, while dealing simultaneously with personal issues reawakened by parenting. All parents, in their efforts to raise, discipline, and nurture children, bring to the present task the sum total of their existence. That is, parents are a product of

"All parents, in their efforts to raise, discipline, and nurture children, bring to the present task the sum total of their existence."

their own past: how they were parented, loved, and disciplined. They are also affected by the type of attachment they developed with significant others. Besides the historical relationships that they have experienced, parents bring with them the losses, trauma, and tragedy from their own pasts. These are what we refer to as echoes from the parents' past. They are faced to some degree by all who raise children. When it comes to foster and adoptive care it is nearly inevitable.

While certainly all parents—birth, step, grand, foster and adoptive—enter the job with echoes from their past, we focus here on echoes in fostering and adopting. These issues may collide with or intersect with issues in the foster or adopted child. In any case, they rarely make parenting any easier, and they call for a very personal form of heroism.

In work with foster and adoptive parents, common echoes include:

1. Infertility issues

2. Attachment relationships with their own parents

3. Relationships with their siblings

4. Unresolved developmental issues

5. Significant losses

6. Exposure to abuse

Disturbed foster and adoptive children have an uncanny knack for discovering and uncovering the unresolved echoes from a parents' past. The child's symptomatic behavior often reflects some unconscious process of pinpointing the parents' Achilles Heel. Interestingly, it is often the ghosts from the child's early history that resonate with the echoes from the adoptive parents. There can be major difficulties, especially if the parent's issues have been unconscious, defended heavily, and are only reawakened by the child's particular issues. We now turn to a discussion of echoes from the parents' past.

"Disturbed foster and adoptive children have an uncanny knack for discovering and uncovering the unresolved echoes from a parents' past."

1. Infertility

Infertility has been mentioned by many writers as a potential echo. Nagging doubts surrounding the couple's infertility may impair a healthy sense of entitlement to the child. Author, Lois Melina, states succinctly that the infertile couple may feel that they are acting against a "divine plan" when they adopt, and that they perhaps were not intended to have children. She adds that if the couple deduces that they, due to infertility, may be defying fate by adopting, then they may feel less certainly that the child "belongs" to them or with them. This may impair their ability to act forcefully with the child through discipline or it may heighten their insecurities and increase a tendency to overprotect their adopted child, as seen in this case study:

> The Kramers were a newly adopting, well-educated couple in their mid-thirties. Childless due to infertility, they had struggled for years with the existential question of whether they were destined to have children or not. Mr. Kramer, in particular, whose low sperm count had been implicated as the cause of infertility, took on the lion's share of responsibility and guilt for the couple's predicament. Mrs. Kramer felt less guilt, but shared a fatalistic perception with her husband: namely, that as a couple they were, in her words, "taunting the gods" by their adoption of Paul, age seven.
>
> In psychotherapy sessions, it was revealed that Mr. Kramer was painfully unable to discipline Paul who had been living with them for eight months. Paul, who had preexisting problems with manipulation and temper tantrums, was accomplished at playing a "victim" role with parents. He was very skilled at exploiting Mr. Kramer's "Achilles' heel," his inability to discipline Paul for misbehavior. Mr. Kramer was effectively stymied by his pity for the child and his tentative and vacillating rules. The underlying feeling seemed to be that he was not meant to have children and was incompetent at reproducing them, therefore he was equally incompetent at raising them. This mostly unconscious feeling was an echo that reverberated through the feeble attempts on Mr. Kramer's part to discipline Paul. That is, Mr. Kramer's self-doubts and re-

*criminations impaired his ability to firmly limit and conse-
quence the child for misbehavior. In response to his adoptive
father's halting parental style, Paul pushed misbehavior further, which seemed to corroborate the doubts of his new father all the more.*

As seen in the this case example, a family echo—specifically related
to infertility—negatively impacted the adoptive father's capacity to
claim, to discipline clearheadedly, and to parent effectively. While
the adoptive parents had been imparted legal rights to Paul, they
had not thoroughly and comfortably claimed him as their own
emotionally. The infertility issue in this case had gone unresolved,
leaving Mr. Kramer in particular as the individual feeling most
puny. Infertility may subtly but powerfully erode self-esteem, confidence, and assertiveness, all of which are important to forthright
parenting. In Mr. Kramer's case the erosion weakened his capacity
to discipline firmly.

Additionally, in psychotherapy sessions the echo was identified
more clearly. Mr. Kramer admitted to having a difficult time in
dealing with Paul as the visible reminder of his infertility. That is,
Paul's very presence raised unpleasant, unwelcome associations.
"Paul's existence in this family confirms my inadequacy as a pro-
genitor." Mr. Kramer had never spoken of these negative associations to his wife, and he had only rarely allowed himself the time
to ponder these feelings, dismissing them as irrational and silly.
Having fairly actively suppressed these "irrational" feelings, Mr.
Kramer was unaware of how these feelings continued to fester and
impact his relationship to Paul. The
negative associations, suppressed,
found expression in a more round-
about, if acceptable, way. Mr. Kramer
dealt with his lack of positive feelings
for Paul by adopting a rather permis-
sive and somewhat neurotically pro-
tective disciplinary posture. The
unexpressed, unconscious sentiment

> "The adoptive father
> dealt with his lack of
> positive feelings for his
> son by adopting a per-
> missive and somewhat
> neurotically protective
> disciplinary posture."

here could be seen as: "Though I feel somewhat hostile and unlov-
ing toward Paul, I can permit him more latitude for his misbehavior, which will convey a guilty love to him."

In view of the infertility issue as an echo that affects parenting, it should be added here that, in general, to parent effectively involves both love and discipline. In particular, correct, measured, and healthy disciplining of our children demands a certain confidence in our abiding love of them. When we are clear in our undying affection for our children, we then can more easily discipline, unhampered by either over-protectiveness or by harshness. Infertility issues unexamined and unresolved may echo through the adoption. In the words of adoption expert, Ken Watson, "Adoption solves childlessness, not infertility." So, this father must resolve these issues while also continuing to parent. Self-healing on the fly.

2. Attachment Relationships to Their Own Parents

Here's another juggling act. Foster and adoptive parents often have to deal with their own attachment issues past and present, while helping their children work through their issues. Parents' unresolved attachment issues can significantly influence parenting. A foster or adoptive parent with a cold, rejecting, and uninvolved mother in his background may be impacted more heavily by a foster or adoptive child who behaves in a cold and withdrawn fashion. Similarly, the foster or adoptive parent who grew up with a clingy, symbiotic mother or father, may be put off by an extremely clingy, needy, dependent foster or adoptive child. In these and many other instances, the foster or adoptive parents' "unfinished business" with their own parents may dictate how they react to certain children. The following case shows a parental echo related to unresolved past relationships.

> *"Foster and adoptive parents often have to deal with their own attachment issues past and present, while helping their children work through their issues."*

> Harvey and Nancy Schmidt were very concerned, experienced foster parents with previous experience in handling troubled youngsters, usually teens. They never intended to adopt any of the children until the arrival of Phillip, a very winning, intelligent foster son, who was relinquished by his biological mother and father soon after placement. Although the Schmidts had

children of their own, now grown and gone, they had all been girls, much to Mr. Schmidt's chagrin. He always felt somewhat outnumbered by the females in the house and had always pined for a son. Mr. Schmidt felt cheated by life in that he had experienced a great deal of noninvolvement and outright emotional abuse from his father, a stern, sometimes volatile man with a chronic drinking problem. With the arrival of Phillip in the home, Mr. Schmidt had somehow felt more interested in foster parenting than ever before. Though Phillip actively spurned the attentions of his foster mother, he left the door open to a relationship to Mr. Schmidt.

Without fully understanding the cause of his heady excitement, Mr. Schmidt enthusiastically jumped into a fathering role with Phillip. They went to baseball games together. They went hunting, fishing, and camping together. Mr. Schmidt made Phillip his long-lost companion, a replacement for the relationship he had never enjoyed with his father or with his daughters. Not surprisingly, Mrs. Schmidt felt somewhat left behind and passed over by her husband and by Phillip as well. When Phillip and Mrs. Schmidt engaged in arguments or any conflicts in the home, Mr. Schmidt almost reflexively came to the boy's defense. This caused a rift between the couple.

What may often develop in situations such as the above is that the child who already feels threatened by intimacy of family life may be totally alarmed by the constant approach of the parent with an urgency to relate to him/her. In Phillip's case, the boy eventually began to remove himself from his adoptive father. Phillip, for example, would not return home from school on time on those days when he and his father were scheduled for an outing together. Mr. Schmidt's reaction was an all-too-familiar feeling of being letdown, cheated, and manipulated. In this case, Mr. Schmidt needed to deal with old feelings entangled with his new and changing relationship to his foster son.

3. Relationship with Their Siblings
Not all echoes are negative. To the contrary, some reverberations from the past are very positive and have the potential to assist fos-

ter or adoptive parents in the task of caring for, attaching to, and parenting troubled children, as seen in the following case:

Mrs. Dinkins was an exceptional foster/adoptive mother who was raising seven special needs children by herself. She was widowed in her early thirties and never remarried; she threw herself into the parenting role with gusto. In getting to know about her past history, the therapist who worked with many of her children discovered that Mrs. Dinkins altruism was a life-long endeavor with roots in her own unique childhood.

Mrs. Dinkins had been the oldest daughter in a family of ten children. She had taken on a parental role of sorts early on, assisting her mother with the younger children, and, in particular, with her youngest brother who was born with severe physical and mental challenges. Mrs. Dinkins spoke fondly of her younger brother, now deceased, and described with obvious pride how she had helped him to cope with his limitations and assisted him in learning rudimentary life skills. Her memories also centered very positively on her mother's constant praise for her dedication to her brother and to the other children.

Though the children who had been placed with Mrs. Dinkins later in her life experienced challenges of a psychological rather than physical/mental nature, Mrs. Dinkins drew strength (and expertise) from positive echoes emanating from her childhood. A care-giver by both disposition and early training, Mrs. Dinkins seemed extremely buoyant and nearly unsinkable emotionally in dealing with highly taxing and troubled children. Her past experience assisted her in accepting traits in children that seemed virtually unchangeable and in taking pride and encouragement from the small, at times almost immeasurable, gains that her foster/adoptive children made in her care. Interestingly, Mrs. Dinkins seemed most gratified in the "baby steps" made by her most incorrigible children.

"Her past experience assisted her in accepting traits in children that seemed virtually unchangeable."

The positive echoes in Mrs. Dinkins world are mentioned here to underscore the often observed fact that past relationships in the foster/adoptive parents' lives can bolster their capacity to parent very difficult children. It makes their heroic efforts easier. Additionally, the incidents, trauma, and tragedy in their early lives may strengthen them and prepare them for the trauma and tragedy in the lives of foster and adoptive children.

4. Unresolved Issues

All parents have their weaknesses. Disturbed, attachment-disordered foster and adoptive children have a remarkable ability to find the parents' "Achilles' heel." If for example, the parents have issues around food and behavior at the table, the child may refuse to eat and sneak food in midnight raids of the refrigerator or pantry. If, on the other hand, the foster or adoptive parents have issues with tidiness, orderliness, and punctuality, the child may divine this and act out accordingly. Specifically, if the parents live by the adage, "Cleanliness is next to godliness," the child will show issues around personal hygiene, bedroom disarray, and general messiness in the home. If the parents are obsessed with being on time, accomplishing as much as possible, and making the proper use of time, then the child is foot-dragging, tardy, and oblivious to time. If the parents struggle with sexual issues and have not resolved their own sexual conflicts (e.g. if they are extremely prudish or sexually inhibited), the child may flaunt sexual behavior in the placement.

> "Disturbed, attachment-disordered foster and adoptive children have a remarkable ability to find the parents' 'Achilles' heel.'"

Is the emergence of specific acting-out behaviors strictly and solely related to the child's mix of temperament and history? Or does the specific manifestation some how merge with the developmental context of the foster or adoptive parents? It is my belief that the disturbed foster or adoptive child's symptoms, behavior patterns, and problematic activity relates to both. Admittedly, the acting-out behaviors mentioned above are strongly, and sometimes totally, brought about because of child factors. On other occasions, however, observations point to the intersection of child factors with parental issues. Here is a case of intersection:

Mr. Wiles was a dedicated and concerned father and husband with grown children and a successful career as a design engineer with a prestigious manufacturing company. Mrs. Wiles, herself an accomplished script writer and former teacher, had also been a very good mother. Although they were well into their forties when they adopted Martin (at age ten), their home study was predictably favorable. Six months into the placement, however, Martin's behavior had deteriorated to the point where the two very exasperated parents were questioning whether to keep Martin. Although Martin had never supposedly shown these specific behavior problems in past foster home placements, after the adoption he exhibited extreme messiness, tardiness, and disorganization. Mr. Wiles expressed that his "pet peeve" was unnecessary untidiness. He himself had been raised with the notion "everything has its place, everything in its place." Mr. Wiles found his carpentry and woodworking tools scattered about the basement and in the backyard. Matthew had "borrowed" them without asking and never returned them to their proper place.

Mrs. Wiles, herself a very organized and orderly parent, found herself in constant battles with Martin over the chaotic situation in his bedroom. She portrayed his bedroom as "room lasagna...there are layers of clean clothes topped by dirty clothes, covered by homework papers, overlaid by more dirty clothes and indistinguishable food stuffs." Mrs. Wiles was not only appalled by the squalor of the room, but also by Martin's apparent inability or unwillingness to learn how to organize the room. It was a constant irritant to her and over time consumed the mother-son relationship. Why had the placement, with all its high resolve, deteriorated to the level of a battleground over hygiene and order? Possibly because Martin has a way of finding the right button to push to open the exit door, the escape hatch out of this home.

The scenario with the Wiles family and Martin depicts an all-too-common discovery. Whether the issues of the parents surround concerns of neatness (as above) or some other focal point, the child's behavior problems erupt seemingly in response. In a different family than the Wiles, Martin's problem behaviors might have centered on very different areas. Indeed, history revealed that Martin had been much more troubled by lying and stealing in the previous foster home placement. Ironically, in that home Martin kept his room respectably tidy. When the foster father's tools came up missing in that home, they were never found again. And, Matthew lied about stealing them. In that foster home, truthfulness was seen as the ultimate family value. Now in the tidy Wiles home, the parents need to confront their Achilles' Heel as they learn to live with Martin.

5. Significant Losses

Every human being experiences loss. Some foster or adoptive parents have experienced losses in their lives that impact how they parent. The loss may have occurred during their childhood and may have involved a death in the family, separation from loved ones, or a painful divorce. Or, the loss may have taken place in adult life. Divorce, death of a parent, or disruptive geographical moves may impact them. One major loss to parents is the death or disappearance of their child. The grief and mourning process these parents may have gone through may lack completeness and resolution. Indeed, some might say that the mourning never resolves completely in such instances. The emotional pain of the loss of offspring may linger and permeate the development of new relationships to foster or adopted children. The most obvious way that the pain influences present relationships is when the child is expected to relieve the pain and to fill the psychological vacuum left by the lost child. A foster or adoptive child's reaction to the parental expectations may be to act out. Especially with at-risk, troubled children, the unspoken demands by the foster or adoptive parents may precipitate a host of behavioral and emotional problems:

> "Some foster or adoptive parents have experienced losses in their lives that impact how they parent."

Mr. Peters was a single, widowed adoptive father of a sibling group of two young boys. He lost his wife and son to a fire a few years before. The tragic losses he had experienced were revealed when he came in for treatment of depression. Mr. Peters also reported that there were significant difficulties with the adoptive boys, who had failed to incorporate into the family he had hoped for. In discussing adoption, Mr. Peters revealed that he and his wife had shared the fantasy of adopting before the tragic fire. Approximately one year after the deaths of his wife and son, he explored the possibility of adoption once again. Within two months the two brothers, ages six and seven, were placed with him. Both boys had been victims of early maltreatment, including physical and sexual abuse, and neglect. They were essentially withdrawn and untrusting children who recoiled from Mr. Peters' friendly overtures.

Psychotherapy with Mr. Peters addressed the deep feelings of guilt that he felt about the death of his loved ones. Although Mr. Peters made a superhuman effort to save his wife and son from the smoke and flames that engulfed their home, he continued to agonize with "survivor guilt." Symptoms clearly defined post traumatic stress disorder. Additionally, Mr. Peters, in psychotherapy, became aware of how he had unconsciously hoped his adoptive sons might fill the void left by his loss. Instead, the boys' own limitations related to past maltreatment combined with Mr. Peters unresolved losses to the detriment of all. The boys felt threatened by the active overtures that Mr. Peters made, while Mr. Peters felt repeatedly rejected by his adoptive sons. His sense of failing his wife and biological son was amplified by his latest "failure."

"If a parent has his own issues with loss, he may increase the severity of the children's corresponding issues with increased demands that the children relate to him."

With many troubled foster and adoptive children, intimacy demands are a threat. Family life is fearsome. Belonging is a harbinger of not-belonging. Attachments are meant to be broken. Children like this are loss-sensitive and often family phobic. If they sense demands for attachment and closeness beyond what they can tolerate—and that may not be much—they balk, act out, and withdraw. If a parent has his own issues with loss, he may increase the severity of the children's corresponding issues with increased demands that the children relate to him.

6. Exposure to Abuse

When it comes to parenting, a parent's history of abuse can help or hurt. If the foster or adoptive parent has been a victim of past abuse, physical or sexual, there may be echoes that resonate through the parenting of maltreated children. The echoes are not always negative, since exposure to abuse may provide insight and empathy that is unsurpassed. In some instances, parents, as a result of their own unfortunate histories, may find their parenting negatively impacted. They may act over-protectively toward children with whose pain they strongly identify. In other instances these parents may feel deeply threatened by their children's behavior problems. This can nix a placement, as we see next.

> Mr. and Mrs. Rudolph had been foster parents for approximately six months when a challenging ten-year-old girl, Carla, was placed with them following allegations of sexual abuse involving the mother's boyfriend. Although the Rudolphs had been successful with brief placements of two previous foster children, the placement with Carla was almost immediately in crisis. Mr. Rudolph, in particular, was appalled by Carla's eroticized behavior. Carla attempted to sit on Mr. Rudolph's lap on the first day of placement, and she, in his words, "hunched" on his leg in a sexual way. Immediately, Mr. Rudolph spoke to his wife and insisted that the child be moved out of the home as soon as possible. Emergency involvement by the caseworker was too late to save the placement. Carla was moved to another foster home a day later.

Unfortunately, it was learned later that Mr. Randolph had himself been a victim of sexual abuse as a child. Fondled and otherwise molested over a number of years by an uncle, Mr. Randolph had never spoken of the abuse to anyone. He struggled over the years within himself, feeling a sense of guilt and responsibility for not having prevented, rebuffed, or somehow terminated the abuse. Having failed to resolve his own guilt feelings, Mr. Rudolph, over time, gradually suppressed the painful memories. The arrival of Carla in the house, along with her overtly seductive behavior toward him, evoked echoes from his past. Once again, Mr. Rudolph felt molested and blame-ridden, as if he had somehow caused the child's sexualized behavior.

Summary Remarks:

In this chapter we have seen that troubled foster and adoptive children can create mayhem in the family. Even with experienced parents, raising a child with significant problems can make the parents look crazy themselves. When the child's problems collide with echoes from the parents' own past, then there can be real struggles. How parents handle the collision demands the courage to face and resolve their own issues, while simultaneously helping their child or children.

In Chapter Five we turn to unorthodox parenting that foster and adoptive parents use to deal with unorthodox problems from the children they are raising.

Chapter Five

Family Interventions

In my opinion, today's foster and adoptive parents are reinventing parenting. They probably have to, what with the caliber of problems children face today. This reinventing takes courage. In this chapter we focus on some unusual parenting approaches used by foster and adoptive parents. In some instances parenting troubled children still comes down to typical, consistent, vanilla-flavored parenting. At other times, however, you need some other flavors, especially when you find yourself on rocky roads. These other flavors include unusual, creative, and off-the-wall approaches—and the courage to use them.

Chapter Five focuses on how genuine, but informal, therapy for many children goes on day-in-day-out in the foster or adoptive home. This informal therapy taps into the powerful teaching and healing influence of family relationships. This chapter also presents a smattering of off-center strategies that families have used to help children. For example, the teenager with an unusual demand: she insisted on a three-, and only three-, year adoption. Then an unusual tale of a young child with mysterious blue lips and what her family did about them. Next, a new invention by a foster father for a child who couldn't sit still at the dinner table: the "Una-Stool." We also outline strategies used with a child who played with matches, and a child who spit in her foster mother's face. Other strategies focus on how to work with a child who can't sleep alone and children who don't know how to contribute around the house. We see how one family dealt with a teen who was going to drop out of an independent living program. Other strategies include working with a child who couldn't accept other children's foibles at the dinner table; assisting a child who was conflicted about growing up and leaving home; intervening with still another who wouldn't stop smoking in his bedroom; and redirecting a child who rebelled against his adoptive parents by reading hate literature. Lastly, we will list a pot pourri of inventive parenting approaches that offer a sense of the breadth and creativity of foster and adoptive parents. First, let's get started with an explanation of informal therapy.

Informal "Therapy" for Foster and Adopted Kids

Traditionally, when we think about therapy or psychotherapy for children, conventional approaches come to mind: play therapy, behavior modification, and family therapy. We recall the trips to the mental health clinic, the wait in the reception area, and the confidential confessional the child enters for his/her "fifty-minute hour."

In this traditional model of mental health involvement, the expert, the change agent, and therapist are one and the same: the mental health professional.

As controversial as this sounds, traditional therapy is often times not a good match for children who live in foster homes, group facilities, special needs adoptive placements, and residential care. In the worst case scenario, conventional psychotherapy and family therapy may inadvertently undermine the stability of placements. At the least, orthodox psychotherapy may offer little to stabilizing the child's life in placement, to confronting acting-out behaviors that threaten the placement, and to addressing relationship issues so often at the core of the child's progress.

Informal therapy builds upon the foster or adoptive parents as **the** resident experts, **the** central change agents, and **the** bona fide, at-home "therapists" for their children. Though they do not hold therapist licenses or counselor's certificates, foster parents, legal risk foster/adoptive parents, group home parents, and special needs adoptive parents must be viewed as the lead members of the therapy team. Rather than being relegated to waiting in the reception area of a mental health clinic, these parents should typically be included in therapy sessions. In that way, issues arising with their children at home become important grist for the therapeutic mill. Strategies for managing the child's acting-out behavior, for fostering better verbalization of emotion, for engendering negotiation and social skills, and for promoting positive relationships and healthier attachments to others are developed by the therapy teams (composed of agency worker, foster or adoptive parents, mental health counselor, and others, as needed).

> *"Informal therapy builds upon the foster or adoptive parents as the resident experts, the central change agents, and the bona fide, at-home "therapists" for their children."*

Let's look at some unusual challenges posed by children and at some atypical strategies used by foster and adoptive parents.

Three-Year Adoption

> Recently, a mental health therapist asked me, "What do I do with a thirteen-year-old girl who wants a three-year adoption?" His client, a female foster child, was free for adoption legally but for some reason was insisting that the only way she'd accept an adoptive placement was with the three-year rider. What was that all about? Why the time limits? How should this be approached?

The reason for this odd request, as best we could figure it, was that the girl would be sixteen at the end of the three-year stint with an adoptive family. At that point she could quit school and search for her birth family.

This nonnegotiable demand communicated that the teen was willing yet resistant and wanted to remain in control. There may have been more to her demand than the desire to search. A multiply-placed youngster, she may have built in her weasel clause, e.g. a way out, a limit on love. Likely, she was opposed to a long-term commitment.

With these thoughts in mind, how should the girl be approached? We could have confronted her about her ambivalence/resistance. But, she might actually have resisted further. Interestingly, it was an experienced adoptive family under consideration for this girl that came up with an off-the-wall suggestion that turned the tide. "Since she is so stubborn, why don't you offer us as a two-year family. Come up short by a year." The mental health therapist announced to the teen at her next therapy session that he had good news and bad news: the good being they'd found a short-term adoptive family, the bad news was they would only commit to two years. If it went well, they would be happy to extend the adoption. As you might expect from a stubborn teenager, the girl's response was an incredulous: "What kind of families do you have out there that refuse to commit for the long haul?"

10,000 Flushes

A foster mother brought her five-year-old daughter to me with a concern: she had blue lips. Thinking this might be a respiratory problem or a circulation disorder, she took her to the family physician. He determined that the girl had been drinking out of the toilet bowl. The blue cleaning agent left her lips that same hue.

The history of the behavior finally emerged. Our little girl's birth parents had cured her of bed-wetting at night by restricting all liquid intake after 6 p.m. Though that proved successful, the girl began wetting during the day. Foolishly the parents determined that restricting fluid intake during the day would also be effective. That meant that our little girl had nothing to drink all day and all night. She was constantly parched. And, as any pet will discover, she found the toilet contained water.

Once the history of the problem was discovered, the foster family devised some strategies that seemed to help. First, for safety sake, they removed the bluing agent from all toilets. Next, they left water out everywhere in pitchers. They constantly asked their foster daughter if she'd like something to drink. They had her carry a canteen full of water wherever she went. Lastly, they bought a helmet with bottle holders built in and tubes running down to her mouth. That way, wherever she went she had the constant weight of available beverages on her head. That eliminated drinking from the toilet.

The One-Legged Stool

An adopting couple in Canada came up with a unique strategy to handle a child with the problem of "aerobic dining habits." This was a boy who was ADHD and who, at six, was a whirling dervish at the dinner table—up, down, up, down all through the meal. The adoptive mother stated that he would reach across the table and grab food from the other children's plates.

"He doesn't have a stomach ulcer, but he's a carrier, eh!" Lamented the adoptive father. "It makes me nervous just watching him. He leans back on his chair, flirting with the law of

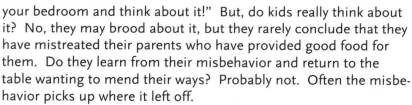

gravity. Once in a blue moon he tips over backwards. But, that doesn't deter him from doing it all over again."

Many children misbehave at the table. Their manners are uncouth. They play with their food. They can be loud, argumentative, rowdy, and boisterous. And, when disruptions like this occur, the quality of family dinners suffer.

A common way to address the problem is to send the child to his room. "Go to your bedroom and think about it!" But, do kids really think about it? No, they may brood about it, but they rarely conclude that they have mistreated their parents who have provided good food for them. Do they learn from their misbehavior and return to the table wanting to mend their ways? Probably not. Often the misbehavior picks up where it left off.

In the adoptive situation with our "aerobic diner" the father came up with a most unusual way of handling the troublesome behavior. He invented a one-legged stool: a padded seat with no back and with a single leg. It was a peg-legged stool, which he dubbed, "The Una-Stool." (Note: Foster and adoptive parents in Tillamook, Oregon or Baraboo, Wisconsin will recognize this as a milking stool.) Positioned on this seat the little boy could swivel in circles, rotate right or left, and tip back and forth. With only one chair leg beneath him, the boy could not stand up or lean forward to reach someone else's plate. If he tried to do that, the chair fell to the ground. He didn't like that and tried to keep control of the chair.

It kept him at his place, seated, but still able to move in a relatively non-disruptive fashion.

Forging New Behavior

Fire-setting is an unsettling and potentially lethal problem in foster and adopted children. There are many varieties of fire-setting ranging from arson to accidental, experimental "playing" with matches.

> Johnny, an eleven-year-old boy raised by his grandfather, had a dangerous fascination with fire. He loved to fiddle with matches and was caught several times with a cigarette lighter in his pocket. Where he found these items, no one knew. But, it was clear that his interest wasn't going to simply disappear.
>
> The grandfather, in response to this problem, bought a forge. He made a point of learning how to operate this himself: lighting it, tending the fire, using the bellows, etc. And, then he tutored Johnny in the same tasks. They forged steel and learned to bend and shape horseshoes for their Quarter Horse. They literally spent hours together fanning flames, heating metal, and pounding white hot horseshoes. It was a hot, sweaty job, but they continued this operation for weeks. Johnny loved the task and seemed to enjoy the companionship. Over time, the match play disappeared completely.

Spitting Mad

Teachers encounter many problems with foster and adopted children during the school day. Even though they endure a mere six hours per day with the children, and while they get weekends off to heal, special education teachers definitely earn their pay. While many teachers are trained to work with troubled youngsters, some of them call foster and adoptive parents for help.

> A treatment foster mother told me about an eight-year-old foster daughter, Bambi, who threw unholy fits at school every Monday morning. The child had visits with her birth parents nearly every weekend. These visits seemed to be chaotic at

best and borderline neglectful at worst. In any case, Bambi
was a basket case on Mondays, and she brought her baskets
to school with her.

On one fateful Monday morning, Bambi went "postal," over-
turning desks, hurling scissors at a fellow student, and attacking
an aide. The teacher asked the aide to evacuate the room with
the five other pupils and make an emergency call to the foster
mother. When the foster mom arrived, she found the teacher
chasing Bambi around the classroom. (Or was it the other way
around?) At that point Bambi began throwing chairs around
and then grabbed and brandished a scissors. The foster mother,
who had training in this, somehow grabbed hold of the child,
disarmed her, and put her down on the floor on her back. Try-
ing to get the child to stop shrieking and thrashing, the foster
mother leaned forward, bringing her face closer and closer to
that of the child whose eyes were clenched shut. She whispered,
"Calm down, Bambi. Take it easy, Bambi." The mother's face
was within point blank range of the child, who suddenly opened
her eyes, saw her target, and spit a—what the foster mother
later described as a "loogie"—at her. The spittle hit the good
woman on the forehead and stuck, hanging suspended between
herself and the child.

Now, honestly, you might wonder what your own reaction would
be in a high stress situation like this. Would you feel like spitting
back? Would you be irate? Would your stomach do flip-flops? Or,
would you make this a teachable moment, instructing the child
about gravity? (That is, what goes up must come down.)

Interestingly, the foster mother reported, "I don't know why I
did this, but I leaned over instantly and kissed Bambi on the
forehead. The tantrum stopped immediately!"

A Down-Filled "Mommy Bag"

For some, sleep is as easy as falling off a log, or at least falling into
bed. For others, the whole experience of sleep is difficult and even
threatening. Sleep demands a certain act of trust, surrender of
control, turning off outward focus and looking inside, slowing

down, letting in a flood of images, memories, and fantasies, and, in the end, a total letting go. With so many troubled foster and adoptive children, none of these tasks come easy, and, indeed, some are nearly impossible.

> One foster/adoptive family discovered that their eleven-year-old adopted daughter refused to sleep in her bed. They found her sleeping by turns under her bed, in a bedroom closet, in the front hall closet, and once, wedged between an upright piano and the living room wall. When bedtime came, this child literally went into hiding. Resultant conversations with the child revealed that she had been repeatedly sexually abused in the night by a series of her birth mother's boyfriends.

While some children make themselves scarce at bedtime, others are frightened to sleep alone. They are not concerned about hiding from us, but rather that we are hidden from their sight. Having experienced various separations and losses, some occurring at night, they seek togetherness when the lights go down. They try to forestall the inevitable separations of darkness, distance, and unconsciousness by traditional means: dragging out the bedtime ritual, dawdling over tooth brushing,

wheedling extra parental time, clinging to parents and crying when they depart. It is the battle of bedtime.

Questions arise over the battle of bedtime: should we insist that children always sleep in their beds and in their bedrooms? Does the child who attempts to insinuate his/her way into the parental bed need to be dissuaded at all costs? Or, are their ways to address the issue other than banishment from the master bedroom? Are there times when exceptions can be made?

> One family addressed a foster child's fear of being alone in his bedroom by allowing the child to sleep in a sleeping bag outside the parent's bedroom. The child called it his "mommy bag." The family felt that the fact that their foster child confided his fears to them was an improvement. They knew that in the past he would have nightmares and remain wide-eyed in his bedroom. This was the same child who as a sick infant was left to lie in a vomit-drenched bed by his birth parents.

Kiddie Workfare

"Have you done your homework?" "Did you clean your room?" "Have you done your chores yet?" "Did you find a summer job?" So many of the struggles parents have with kids center on work, chores, and pitching in. The struggle centers on instilling a good work ethic in the children and adolescents. Related issues are: motivation to work, commitment to finishing what is started, helping out and doing one's share, being part of the family by working cooperatively, pride in a job well done, interest in working for and with others, and achieving self-sufficiency via earned income. These are issues that many foster and adoptive parents emphasize with their children. These parents recognize the value of hard work, and they rightfully want to pass that on to their children.

Many troubled foster and adoptive children have not learned any work ethic. Growing up in homes where work was scarce, motivation waned, and inconsistency reigned supreme, these youngsters do not understand the joys of work and the confidence that good work habits impart. How do we take a child who is work phobic and help him along?

One foster father had the answer for Timmy, age eleven. With this boy he had two running battles: the first, Timmy played his hip-hop music too loud; and second, his chores never got done. The dad combined these two battles to produce solutions for both. Specifically, he told Timmy that he could play his hip-hop loudly on Saturday mornings while he completed his chores: cleaning his bathroom, picking up and vacuuming his bedroom, and folding and sorting his laundered clothes. He had an hour to do it all. If he wanted to work slowly while he listened fine. If he wanted to quickly finish chores and then luxuriate to the sounds of screaming, that was okay too. It didn't matter to the foster father who planned to stuff his ears with cotton for an hour each week.

Better To Give Than Receive

Nationally, independent living programs focusing on transitioning foster children into independent young adults are all the rage.

Sylvia, age seventeen, had been enrolled in "Project Moving On," an independent living program in a Northwestern state, to prepare her for life on her own. From an impoverished background, she had never enjoyed many "creature comforts" until she entered the program. Provided with a nice apartment, a stipend to live on, and a job coach, Sylvia was, in her own words, "livin' large." With help she found a part-time job that paid better than minimum wage. On paper things were going well. While she should have been enjoying this exciting period of independence, Sylvia instead worried obsessively about her birth family. She felt guilty that as she snoozed comfortably, her siblings were still sleeping on the hard floor. Although provided with a stipend to live on, she felt guilty about using the money for her own needs, thinking that she was being wasteful or showing off her new-found "wealth."

Her misgivings about livin' large while her biological family was still living small held her back from benefiting from the program. Sylvia began to drift away from job training, showing up irregularly for sessions. She talked with her job coach about quitting altogether and returning home to help support her family. (Historically, Sylvia had been a responsible caregiver in her family of origin.) She had a true concern for family members and worried about their entrenched poverty. She sincerely wanted to help them out by leaving the program and returning home to live, work, and contribute financially.

A feature of "Project Move Up" was that it paid Sylvia's monthly rent directly to the landlord. A living stipend for groceries was provided directly to Sylvia. An additional monthly sum of more than $100 dollars was deposited into a savings account that Sylvia would not be able to access until she had successfully completed the independent living program.

Sylvia's foster parents, who still remained a part of her world, had an idea. They suggested that program staff assist Sylvia in creative use of her $100 dollar monthly savings fund. They felt that if they negotiated with Sylvia about the use of this money that it would allay her anxieties and reduce her guilt feelings. In the end, they suggested that Sylvia could save the $100 per month as a future nest egg for her family. They helped her to set up a target amount to save and successfully encouraged her to re-involve herself in her own program.

The Infernal Sound of Chewing

A foster family had daily uproar at the breakfast, lunch, and supper table. While they felt that sharing a meal as a family was a good idea, in practice it was mayhem because of Flora, their fourteen-year-old adopted daughter. Flora couldn't handle the sound of chewing, lip-smacking, or talking with mouths-full-of-food, that the three foster brothers were prone to. The boys were a young sibling group with likely fetal alcohol effects. Ages five, six, and eight, they were hyperactive, loud, squirmy, messy, and impolite at the table. It drove Flora crazy!

Flora's history before adoption included the usual abuse, neglect, and moves from foster placement to foster placement. But the relationship to her family of origin was most telling. Flora, the oldest of five children, was frequently in the role of mother surrogate, e.g. she was a parentified child. As such, she was expected to keep her younger siblings quiet and well-behaved around the house and specifically at the dinner table. If they acted up, she was punished.

That's where the problem came in her adoptive home. Flora could not let go of her parental role and remained obsessed about keeping the other kids in line. This was an impossible task even for the adoptive parents, let alone for a fourteen-year-old girl. "Sit down! Sit down! SIT DOWN!!!" Flora would instruct them loudly. "Mom, Dad, they're eating with their mouths open," she would tattle. In her attempt to settle things down, Flora became the biggest problem of all. One of her biggest pet peeves was the sound of the other children chewing, smacking their lips, and rattling their silverware against the plates.

For their part, the foster parents grew increasingly rattled and exasperated. They tried conventional ways to convey to Flora that she did not have to worry about controlling the younger children—to no avail. So, they tried the unconventional.

They placed Flora in charge (yet, under parent supervision) of the children during prescribed dining exercises. First they had Flora ask the children to eat with exaggerated crudeness complete with loud smacking and chewing. She then encouraged the children to speak loudly with their mouths stuffed with food. Following five or so minutes of this "rude and crude" dining exercise, Flora was asked to encourage the opposite: a quiet exercise during which the children were expected to eat properly, chewing with mouths closed, sitting on chairs without squirming, and keeping their hands to themselves. The parents helped out when the younger children didn't follow instructions, teaming up with Flora in her attempts to gain compliance. The primary purpose of the exercise was to de-sensitize Flora to the commotion at the table. The secondary purpose of the exercise was to teach her that the foster parents would help her in her task of keeping the kids in line. Eventually this would set the stage for Flora relinquishing more and more control to the foster parents. In the end, the foster parents found themselves totally in charge at the table, as Flora watched with a look of amusement.

Along with setting-up the dining exercises, which became lighthearted and game-like activities, the foster parents explained to Flora why she acted the way she did with the younger children. They tried to give her insight into her historic role.

I Can't "Weight" to Leave Home

A nineteen-year-old adopted son, Viktor, talked about wanting to move out on his own. At the same time, his family, the Borges, noticed that he began gorging himself with food, gaining forty pounds in three months. History showed that Viktor was sorely neglected in an overseas orphanage from birth to five years of age. He had fixated on food, stealing food and gorging food for several years after his adoption at ten, but the problem subsided until recently.

While Viktor boasted about how great it would be to move out and "party, smoke, and drink," there was an underlying anxiety about growing up and emancipating from the family. Indeed, the adoptive parents agreed that Viktor was very emotionally immature, e.g. about a 13- or 14- year old. Intelligence tests placed Viktor in the low average range of functioning. He was quite impulse-ridden and concrete, not transferring what he learned on day one to day two. The family doctor who medicated Viktor with Concerta for hyperactivity felt that the sudden weight gain was psychologically driven, not physically based.

The adoptive parents approached the weight problem in a very prudent way. First, they avoided criticizing Viktor, instead they talked with him about emotions he might feel as he got ready to leave home. They speculated that he might be excited but terrified of leaving. They vocalized that his body was saying "no" while his words were saying "yes" to the issue of leaving home. The foster parents assumed that Viktor's recent weight gain might be communicating the fear that he would not have enough food when he moved out. With his orphanage background, he may have bulked up for what he unconsciously feared would be a period of starvation, physically and emotionally. The foster mother wondered too if Viktor put on the excess weight so that no one could physically shove him out the front door of his adoptive home.

As time passed the adoptive parents adopted another approach. Since Viktor would not verbalize his fears and conflicts about leaving home, the parents deliberately became neurotic about it for him. The parents adopted the role of worriers, frequently vocalizing their concerns about the leave-taking. They began to speak the unspeakable for Viktor, and though he denied the feelings of worry himself, he seemed to listen to the adoptive parents' worries. Vicarious learning you might call it. As Viktor's move from the home came closer, his adoptive parents reassured him that they would remain in contact with him and that they expected him to come home often to reconnect with them. By this time Viktor had peeled off about twenty-five pounds, but asked if he could take the family's extra microwave with him.

Smokin' in the Boy's Room

Trevor, a fifteen-year-old adopted boy insisted on chewing tobacco and smoking in his room and bathroom. His parents confronted him but he denied violating the rules, even though the smell of smoke wafted through the air. Trevor seemed to derive some satisfaction out of being caught and then debating the issue. The adoptive parents became increasingly upset by his repeated lying and denials; in fact the untruths upset them more than the rebellious use of tobacco products.

The adoptive parents came up with an unusual intervention for Trevor. They told him that he could smoke, but not on the property, which was a 200-acre farm. Throughout the day they would offer to give him a lift to the edge of the property for a "smoking session." He was equipped with his pack of cigarettes and a walkie-talkie to call for a ride back home. From the convenience of their home, the parents could watch Trevor puffing away on his cigarettes. While this new intervention was employed several, if not many, times each day, the adoptive parents ceased asking about the taboo smoking within the house. If they smelled smoke, they immediately offered Trevor a ride to the "South Forty."

Things got interesting when Trevor would be asked—just as he turned on his favorite TV show—to go for a ride to his smoking destination. That wasn't convenient for him, but, with some complaint he went, "Do I have to smoke right now?" I think you can see where the family was going with this unorthodox approach. You might wonder how soon the arguments would change to "You can't make me smoke!"

Skinhead Kid and Flower Children Parents

Cici, a bright fourteen-year-old girl, had been adopted by her parents when she was four. She was the only child to this baby boomer couple who were extremely tolerant, liberal minded, and non-judgmental. (The parents described themselves as grown up "flower children" from the 60's who valued acceptance of diversity.) Ironically, Cici's chosen form of adolescent rebellion was to become in their words, "a skinhead wanna-be." She read hate literature, and books on racism became her passion. She viewed herself as a white supremacist. Of course, the parents were appalled. How could their live-and-let-live, "rainbow coalition" approach to life be so flagrantly disregarded? Fascinating that the ultimate test of their all-accepting philosophy was: Can you accept a budding hatemonger under your roof?

After talking with their adoptive parent support group, the parents began reading the hate literature that Cici left strewn about the house. They asked questions about it and made their own observations, quoting liberally from the books. In fact they researched the literature on the subject and suggested further reading for Cici. In a way, they stole her rebellion away from her.

Reparenting the Unfed Baby Inside the Child

Cory, a five-year-old boy with a history of neglect and abandonment, was left for hours in his crib with baby bottles tossed in with him. Essentially, he was left to feed and fend for himself.

After taking Cory into her home, his single foster mother found that a monthly respite weekend helped her to care for this exhaustingly needy kindergartner. But, at the end of a break, Cory would predictably throw a fit or act stubborn and withdrawn for a few days. To address this behavior, the caseworker suggested to the foster mother that she respond by withdrawing herself. While she found that unnatural and uncomfortable, she went along with the recommendation temporarily. After a week of mutual withdrawal, however, the foster mother resorted to holding and rocking Cory, whose withdrawal immediately evaporated. The foster mother felt much more comfortable using the loving approach with the little boy.

Potpourri of Strategies

I am continually amazed by the creativity and instincts that foster and adoptive parents bring to their loving work with children. The examples of creative parenting are almost endless, and it would be impossible to list, let alone describe them all. Still, I want to mention a few other eye-catching strategies that may provide a glimpse of how creative parents have become.

A foster mother, concerned about her foster son's storing of knives under his pillow, equipped him with a bedside whistle that he could blow to summon her. His knife collection, she determined, made him feel safe but indicated that he thought he alone could keep himself safe. The whistle brought her into the act. Now, she could help him feel safe.

A single foster dad fought the natural tendency to get angry about his missing tools. He found that his foster son had stockpiled them in his room, specifically between his mattresses. The father put the boy in charge of the tools, making the bedroom into a U-Rent-It facility. The boy, a control freak, was entrusted with logging tools in and out as other family members needed them.

An adoptive mom addressed temper tantrum problems by instructing the child in the proper way to throw fits. It became more of a coordination exercise with legs and arms moving in concert.

Foster parents coped with a young girl, who was constantly approaching strangers, by introducing themselves to the strangers as foster care recruiters.

A foster father found himself forced to throw a surprise birthday party for his eighteen-year-old foster son. No one had ever celebrated his birthday before. As the scheduled event grew closer, the young man—so excited or frightened—was close to blowing out of the placement. The foster father wisely threw a surprise party several days early to make a "pre-emptive strike." The father commented, "I wasn't going to let him destroy the opportunity for others to celebrate his life."

"I wasn't going to let him destroy the opportunity for others to celebrate his life."

One creative adoptive mother invented an approach she called, "Parenting By Memo." This grew out of negative encounters with her teenaged adopted son, whose notion of communication was a grunt, a shrug, and a quick exit from the room. She found that if she wrote questions to him on paper, he would answer back in writing. One curious finding was that if she ever praised him in her written memo, he would read it, but immediately crumple it up and toss it away. That gave the mother another idea: when she wanted to praise him, she would compose her thoughts on paper, crumple it up, and lob it in his direction. Wouldn't you know, her son would un-crumple the paper and read her positive words.

A foster mother, who was physically assaulted almost daily by two school-aged foster daughters, wore a complete hockey outfit with pads, shin guards, and helmet to protect herself and to distract the children.

One adoptive father fed his eating-disordered children four meals each day, the latest of which was served at 9 p.m. (e.g. bedtime). He found that this reduced nightly foraging for food.

Whenever their angriest foster son threw a full-blown temper tantrum, the rest of the family gathered in the kitchen to eat ice cream. Curiosity about where everyone had gone and a love of any flavor ice cream prompted the angry son to abort the tantrum and join in the fun.

Summary Remarks:

In this chapter we have focused on unorthodox parenting used by foster and adoptive parents who are confronted with unusual, over-the-top behavior problems. As seen by some of the interventions parents have used, it doesn't hurt to be creative when it comes to the most challenging problems. In a sense, foster and adoptive parents have had to reinvent parenting strategies when it comes to the caliber of difficulties they face with special needs children. I believe invention is the hallmark of the brave.

Afterword

I entitled this book Small Feats because the frequently slow, incremental, and often quite private accomplishments of foster and adoptive parents may, to the untrained eye, appear tiny and inconsequential. But, in actuality being a foster or adoptive parent is NO small feat.

> feat (fet) n. [L. factum, a deed]
> an act or accomplishment showing
> unusual daring, skill, and endurance.

I believe it takes unusual daring, skill, and endurance to be a foster or adoptive parent. Daring, courage, bravery—whatever you'd like to call it—starts with the decision to foster or adopt and builds upon itself over time. Skill—yes, atypical parenting skills, bags upon bags of helpful parenting approaches, and hours of continuing education build over time and may, in the end, look very different than conventional parenting skills. And, lastly there is endurance—stamina, tenacity, commitment—without which daring and skill crash and burn.

This book has barely scratched the surface of parental heroics I've witnessed over the years. Other areas that demand heroism are:

- Dealing with public misconceptions about fostering and adopting.

- Contending with birth family issues.

- Coping with school, welfare, correctional, court, and mental health systems.

- Living with the ever present specter of false allegations.

- Struggling with doubts that only parents know and especially parents of children for whom easy answers do not exist.

- Braving personal issues that arise in each of us as we parent.

- Wrestling with heart-wrenching decisions such as temporarily placing your child in another home, residential facility, or psychiatric hospital; or coming to the conclusion that you must permanently remove your foster or adoptive child from your home.

Lastly, some parting thoughts about heroism: Heroism is not synonymous with victory or success. Heroism is not always one big thing but perhaps many small things. Heroism comes in many sizes and shapes. It might be heroic to have raised three hundred foster children over a twenty year span. It may also have been heroic to have raised one. Thank you for your everyday heroics and unsung accomplishments!

Richard J. Delaney